2000 Would You Rather Questions

Rock Star

Never speak to your family again or never get married?

Married

Give up your favorite food for a year or give up candy forever?

Favorite Food

Date a movie star or rock star?

Pet unicorn or pet dragon?

Dragon

Fly a kite in a rainstorm or walk bare feet on hot coals?

Hot Coals

Hitchhike with strangers cross country or get cross country by train hopping?

Train Hopping

Bit by a vampire or a dog with rabies?

Vampire

Follow us on social media!

Tag us and use #piccadillyinc in your posts
for a chance to win monthly prizes!

This edition published by Piccadilly (USA) Inc.

Piccadilly (USA) Inc.
12702 Via Cortina, Suite 203
Del Mar, CA 92014
USA

10 9 8 7 6 5 4 3 2 1

Printed in China

ISBN-13: 978-1-62009-614-7

1 **WYR** give up your favorite food for a year or give up candy forever?

2 **WYR** live in a windmill or lighthouse?

3 **WYR** be an angel on your friend's shoulder or a devil on your enemy's shoulder?

4 **WYR** eat an entire jar of olives or sauerkraut in 15 minutes?

5 **WYR** get blindsided at work or blindsided in love?

6 **WYR** write and have a best-selling book published or star in a hit blockbuster movie?

7 **WYR** think with your right brain or left brain?

8 **WYR** have a plant or goldfish that talks to you?

9 **WYR** have your mouth freeze with a stupid smile or your eyes freeze crossed?

10 **WYR** take cooking lessons from a celebrity chef or piano lessons from an acclaimed musician?

11 **WYR** have Stan Lee or Kevin Smith create your own comic book character?

12 **WYR** get a tattoo of a cartoon character or a tattoo of the face of a celebrity you like?

13 **WYR** eat ice cream every day for a year or go without ice cream for two years?

14 **WYR** have lunch with an influential billionaire or with your celebrity crush?

15 **WYR** have a jacuzzi in your bedroom or a secret room in your house?

16 **WYR** eat ice cream every day for a year or go without ice cream for two years?

17 **WYR** own your own sports team on a losing streak or own a successful chain of restaurants?

18 **WYR** go to an indoor concert or outdoor concert?

19 **WYR** face your worst fear head on or confess your greatest sins online and it go viral?

20 **WYR** eat falafel balls or meatballs?

21 **WYR** drink water from a glacier or a running spring?

22 **WYR** give up watching movies the rest of your life or never ever read another book?

23 **WYR** donate an organ to a friend in need or sell one to a stranger for tons of money?

24 **WYR** have a pet unicorn or have a pet dragon?

25 **WYR** find a way or make a way?

26 **WYR** be able to record your thoughts or your dreams while you sleep?

27 **WYR** fight the superhero Captain America or fight the villain The Joker?

28 **WYR** never speak to your family again or never get married?

29 **WYR** earn a Pulitzer or be given a medal of honor for a heroic act?

30 **WYR** enter an archery competition or be challenged to a duel?

31 **WYR** be a famous soap opera star or be given the chance to direct a major motion picture?

32 **WYR** work with dead people in a mortuary or work in the busiest ER trauma unit in the world?

33 **WYR** learn how to fly a helicopter or learn how to fly a plane?

34 **WYR** play strip poker with strangers or truth or dare with your enemies?

35 **WYR** only watch Marvel movies or only watch DC Comic movies?

36 **WYR** have a popcorn kernel stuck in your throat or a toothpick break between your teeth?

37 **WYR** break a bone in your foot or hand?

38 **WYR** put your head in a lion's or crocodile's mouth?

39 **WYR** spend your time wisely or just live in the moment?

40 **WYR** attend a dayglow or foam party?

41 **WYR** put a spider or ice cubes down your boo's shirt?

42 **WYR** make a mean person cry or a sweet person laugh?

43 **WYR** have a pinball machine or Pac Man arcade machine for your home?

44 **WYR** hang out with Cookie Monster or Captain Crunch?

45 **WYR** someone hack your bank account or your Facebook account?

46 **WYR** wet the bed or your significant other wet the bed so you can laugh?

47 **WYR** divulge family secrets or details of your love life in your tell-all book?

48 **WYR** have annoying friends who are loyal or cool friends that are shady?

49 **WYR** get lost in New York or Los Angeles?

50 **WYR** talk like SpongeBob or Woody?

51 **WYR** have computer commands for your life or an eraser for your life?

52 **WYR** discover a new island or new civilization?

53 **WYR** have a sports car with or without a convertible top?

54 **WYR** go water skiing or snow skiing?

55 **WYR** have uncontrollable blinking or have your nose flare nonstop?

56 **WYR** your sneeze sound like a siren or a fog horn?

57 **WYR** workout with kettle bells or free weights?

58 **WYR** your tongue turn purple or your lips turn blue?

59 **WYR** have a pet chinchilla or sugar glider?

60 **WYR** lick a salt lick after a cow or suck a honeysuckle after a hummingbird?

61 **WYR** swing on a porch swing or tire swing?

62 **WYR** blow bubbles that play music when they pop or turn into pennies when they pop?

63 **WYR** obsess about your image or let it go?

64 **WYR** take classes you find interesting or ones you think you'll need?

65 **WYR** be a deal maker or a heart breaker?

66 **WYR** risk everything for love or risk everything for a chance at success?

67 **WYR** have all your teeth fall out at once or all your hair?

68 **WYR** attend the Olympics in its entirety or go to a Super Bowl game?

69 **WYR** have chicken nuggets or chicken strips?

70 **WYR** abolish war or find a cure for every type of cancer?

71 **WYR** be reincarnated as an eagle or a lion?

72 **WYR** have a robot servant or a real life personal assistant?

73 **WYR** be trapped on a desert island with your significant other or a survivalist?

74 **WYR** take the road less travelled or follow in others' footsteps?

75 **WYR** run errands in public in slippers and a robe or shower cap and face mask?

76 **WYR** spend 24 hours on the subway or public bus people watching?

77 **WYR** know the exact time and place you'll die or have the option to choose how you will die?

78 **WYR** eat a cantaloupe or avocado skin?

79 **WYR** be an infamous black-hat hacker or the world's best pick-pocket?

80 **WYR** go on an archaeological dig and find a fossil or go gold mining and find some gold?

81 **WYR** be single for a year (this includes no dating) or go on bad dates for a year straight?

82 **WYR** try and train an elephant or a tiger?

83 **WYR** sunbathe nude on a public beach or have a nude scene in a Broadway play?

84 **WYR** date a movie star or rock star?

85 **WYR** hitchhike with strangers across country or get cross country by train hopping?

86 **WYR** fight off an anaconda or a crocodile?

87 **WYR** learn how to carve wood or forge swords?

88 **WYR** teach aerobics or yoga?

89 **WYR** play a hardcore game of kickball or volleyball?

90 **WYR** name your child after a family member or someone who inspires you?

91 **WYR** drink soda from a can or glass bottle?

92 **WYR** get rid of pesticides or growth hormones in food?

93 **WYR** jump like a kangaroo or have the speed of a Mako shark in water?

94 **WYR** eat sundaes with or without a cherry?

95 **WYR** eat more vegetables or fruit?

96 **WYR** go back five years or skip ahead five years in your life?

97 **WYR** hang glide or windsurf?

98 **WYR** kiss a gecko or June bug?

99 **WYR** grub Big Macs or Quarter Pounders?

100 **WYR** watch the Summer Olympics or Winter Olympics?

101 **WYR** have a duck that oinks or a pig that quacks?

102 **WYR** have a squeeze of lime or lemon?

103 **WYR** text only in GIFs or emojis?

104 **WYR** Google yourself or your ex?

105 **WYR** eat broccoli or cauliflower?

106 **WYR** have butterscotch or toffee?

107 **WYR** tie-dye your hair or only wear tie-dye outfits?

108 **WYR** have pizza rolls or pizza bagels?

109 **WYR** control your joystick to your video game by using your foot or mouth?

110 **WYR** have more followers on Twitter or Instagram?

111 **WYR** shop exclusively at Old Navy or H&M?

112 **WYR** wear one of your dad's shirts or your mom's sweaters?

113 **WYR** have cornbread or garlic bread?

114 **WYR** have fish sticks or fresh fish?

115 **WYR** cannonball or dive into a pool?

116 **WYR** view the world as a stage or a playground?

117 **WYR** have creamy or chunky peanut butter?

118 **WYR** learn about secrets that inspired conspiracy theories or become part of a secret society?

119 **WYR** try and survive a zombie apocalypse or a real-life Purge?

120 **WYR** try and attempt Mt. Everest or compete in the Alaskan Iditarod Race?

121 **WYR** learn more about your grandparents or your great grandparents?

122 **WYR** meet Abraham Lincoln or Ghandi?

123 **WYR** perform the ALS ice bucket or ALS pepper challenge?

124 **WYR** bribe someone or blackmail someone to get what you want?

125 **WYR** go on a treasure hunt around the globe or trace your family history?

126 **WYR** attend a séance or a Native American sweat ceremony?

127 **WYR** charter a single engine plane or helicopter?

128 **WYR** eliminate the mob or eliminate the cartel?

129 **WYR** save a person's life or win the lottery?

130 **WYR** tell your best friend in person you no longer like them or just stop talking to them?

131 **WYR** be a visionary or an inventor?

132 **WYR** be trapped in a snowstorm for a week or try and outrun a tornado in your car?

133 **WYR** hang out with wild Miley Cyrus or the *Hanna Montana* version of Miley?

134 **WYR** drive a Ford Mustang or Chevy Camaro?

135 **WYR** dye your hair the color you hate the most for a year or shave your head bald once?

136 **WYR** never go inside another nightclub or never go inside another bar?

137 **WYR** teach driver's ed or CPR to teenagers?

138 **WYR** have a maid or personal chef for the rest of your life?

139 **WYR** retire early at 40 and live in an arctic climate or retire at 65 and live in a tropical climate?

140 **WYR** have a reputation for being a liar or for being promiscuous?

141 **WYR** have hair down to your ankles or be totally bald?

142 **WYR** bring back an extinct species or have a mythical creature exist?

143 **WYR** give up all technology for a week or give up only social media for a month?

144 **WYR** sketch or color in coloring books?

145 **WYR** go the extra mile or pull a rabbit out of your hat?

146 **WYR** have Chewbacca or Robin as your sidekick?

147 **WYR** channel surf or DVR all your shows?

148 **WYR** do 3-D or flat puzzles?

149 **WYR** caramel or mocha Frappuccino?

150 **WYR** pet sit or babysit?

151 **WYR** play keep away or tetherball?

152 **WYR** play marbles or jacks?

153 **WYR** eat Reese's Peanut Butter Cups or Reese's Pieces?

154 **WYR** eat chicken feet or pig knuckles?

155 **WYR** lose the ability to think quick or think under pressure?

156 **WYR** have lips the texture of a coconut or cat's tongue?

157 **WYR** transform into a vampire or be a vampire hunter?

158 **WYR** have a lion or a bear's roar?

159 **WYR** have chapped lips or chapped hands?

160 **WYR** smell like strawberries or peaches?

161 **WYR** be a minimalist or maximalist?

162 **WYR** live near railroad tracks or a busy airport?

163 **WYR** get bored easily or be easily entertained?

164 **WYR** your smartphone print 3-D images or all your photos instantly?

165 **WYR** eat a dead worm or one that's alive?

166 **WYR** get your head stuck in a fence or your body stuck in an airshaft?

167 **WYR** answer trick questions or brain teasers?

168 **WYR** have egg salad or tuna salad?

169 **WYR** see a merman or a female Yeti?

170 **WYR** give up sex for a year or your cell phone for a year?

171 **WYR** find an old undeveloped roll of film or an old family video you haven't seen yet?

172 **WYR** have very fat arms with skinny legs or vice versa?

173 **WYR** have your own TV show on Netflix or HBO?

174 **WYR** plan a wedding for your BFF or plan a major birthday party for your significant other?

175 **WYR** explore the Black Hole to see what's on the other side or try and live on another planet?

176 **WYR** fantasize about food or materialistic things?

177 **WYR** have a high profile or lowkey job?

178 **WYR** get revenge on your enemy or your ex?

179 **WYR** keep playing this "would you rather game" or go to sleep?

180 **WYR** have very fat arms with skinny legs or vice versa?

181 **WYR** spend the rest of your life as a circus clown or a street performer?

182 **WYR** lose your ability to feel any emotion or lose your taste buds?

183 **WYR** wear glasses the rest of your life whether you need them or not or give up pizza forever?

184 **WYR** have a high profile or lowkey job?

185 **WYR** fantasize about food or materialistic things?

186 **WYR** only ever be able to use sign language to speak or walk backwards the rest of your life?

187 **WYR** never celebrate your birthday again or never drink alcohol again?

188 **WYR** throw out a pitch at the World Series or sing the National Anthem at the Super Bowl?

189 **WYR** have a picnic with a dying relative or a famous person you admire?

190 **WYR** read the journal of JFK or MLK Jr.?

191 **WYR** be attacked by a flock of seagulls or try and outrun a stampede of horses?

192 **WYR** be best friends with a famous shoe designer or jean designer?

193 **WYR** trip and fall in front of an audience or in front of someone hot?

194 **WYR** get a shoulder or foot massage?

195 **WYR** have grape jelly or strawberry jam?

196 **WYR** be more logical or reasonable?

197 **WYR** have good karma or send bad karma to someone?

198 **WYR** eat raw cookie dough or cake batter?

199 **WYR** be called an airhead or dork?

200 **WYR** create a new mode of transportation or a new sports league?

201 **WYR** have the wisdom of Yoda or Confucius?

202 **WYR** dill pickles or sweet pickles?

203 **WYR** go to prom or homecoming again?

204 **WYR** feel justified or vindicated?

205 **WYR** find something valuable you lost or fix something valuable that was broken?

206 **WYR** see Oprah or Arnold Schwarzenegger as the next US President?

207 **WYR** sense danger or sense money?

208 **WYR** eat Cracker Jacks or Crunch 'N Munch?

209 **WYR** have Junior Mints or York Peppermint Patties?

210 **WYR** find a magic wand or a book of spells?

211 **WYR** eat a whole bag of marshmallows or whole jar of peanut butter at once?

212 **WYR** wear neckties or bow ties?

213 **WYR** wear hoops or studs?

214 **WYR** your friend yell at you or ignore you when they're mad at you?

215 **WYR** drive an amphibious vehicle or a hovercraft?

216 **WYR** meet in the middle or always get your way?

217 **WYR** wet your pants or vomit on your shoes in public?

218 **WYR** ride a gondola or a trolley?

219 **WYR** have a peg leg or hook for a hand?

220 **WYR** only speak in one liners or only quote movies?

221 **WYR** visit Wakanda or Zamunda?

222 **WYR** be covered in bees or spiders?

223 **WYR** bring back Michael Jackson or Prince from the dead?

224 **WYR** be a genie in a bottle or a wizard?

225 **WYR** pose nude for a class of art students or pose centrefold for a nude magazine?

226 **WYR** have a jiggly face or a face that doesn't move?

227 **WYR** have your own epic tree house or your own CrossFit studio?

228 **WYR** hang out with Frankenstein or The Wolfman?

229 **WYR** have unlimited gift cards to a clothing store or electronic store?

230 **WYR** be physically weak or mentally weak?

231 **WYR** rock a mohawk hairstyle or wear platform shoes with every outfit for a year?

232 **WYR** have a self-cleaning house or a laundry fairy to take care of all your clothes?

233 **WYR** attend the last supper with Jesus or throw a dinner party for the current U.S. President?

234 **WYR** have swollen hands or feet?

235 **WYR** wear pink every day for a year or never wear jewelry (includes wedding ring) again?

236 **WYR** be on house arrest forever or serve 10 years in solitary confinement?

237 **WYR** be the smartest person in the world or the richest?

238 **WYR** go a year without music or a year without TV?

239 **WYR** drown your popcorn in melted butter or cover your ice cream with sprinkles?

240 **WYR** give up coffee for a year or go without brushing your teeth for a year?

241 **WYR** walk home in a downpour or be trapped in the cab ride from hell on your way home?

242 **WYR** have your mom or your dad pick out your clothes?

243 **WYR** achieve a deeper understanding or a higher learning?

244 **WYR** create a list of life hacks or list of goals?

245 **WYR** have a lifetime supply of love or have a lifetime supply of gas for all of your cars?

246 **WYR** have world peace or have any and all cancer types wiped out forever?

247 **WYR** never use toilet paper again or wear wrinkled clothes forever?

248 **WYR** have a bowling alley or basketball court in your backyard?

249 **WYR** never wear shorts or socks again?

250 **WYR** get hit by water from a fireman's hose or from an elephant's trunk?

251 **WYR** be footloose and fancy free or just free?

252 **WYR** have a bunny's nose or tail?

253 **WYR** have a *Maze Runner* or *Hunger Games* experience?

254 **WYR** have ants in your pants or a grub worm in your ear?

255 **WYR** go back in time 1,000 years or go forward 1,000 years?

256 **WYR** have a splinter you can't get out or a seed embedded in your gums?

257 **WYR** be a park ranger or a game warden?

258 **WYR** eat Jell-O made from baby spit or sugar cookies topped with dandruff?

259 **WYR** pick your battles or fight all the battles that come your way?

260 **WYR** be scared of the number 13 or afraid of the dark?

261 **WYR** smell like a sewer or raw onion?

262 **WYR** be competitive or commanding?

263 **WYR** drink powdered milk or can milk?

264 **WYR** groom a cat with your tongue or brush your dog with your hairbrush?

265 **WYR** eat ice cream topped pizza or ice cream topped with rabbit poop?

266 **WYR** wear a scarf or gloves?

267 **WYR** shake things up or fly under the radar?

268 **WYR** stronger arms or legs?

269 **WYR** never take your sunglasses off or never take your hat off?

270 **WYR** only be allowed to speak in slang or never use slang words again?

271 **WYR** lose your sense of smell or taste?

272 **WYR** dream in 3-D or have fewer nightmares?

273 **WYR** climb Jack's beanstalk or fix Humpty Dumpty's cracked shell?

274 **WYR** drink out of a complete stranger's glass or eat your own booger?

275 **WYR** be able to erase people's memory or predict their future?

276 **WYR** get to a party late or too early?

277 **WYR** see a cow jump over the moon or see the man in the moon?

278 **WYR** drink a cup of your significant other's spit or eat one live cockroach?

279 **WYR** have an egg head or be a goober?

280 **WYR** get hypnotized when you look at the moon or sleepwalk when you hear a bell?

281 **WYR** lose a leg but live until 90 or keep your legs and die at 65?

282 **WYR** get head to toe tattoos of your choosing or get really bad botched plastic surgery?

283 **WYR** own the real DeLorean or Batmobile?

284 **WYR** be rebuilt as part machine or part animal if you had a devastating accident?

285 **WYR** have 100 boxes of Girl Scout Cookies or 100 dollars right now?

286 **WYR** have unlimited music downloads for a lifetime or free massages for a year?

287 **WYR** sleep in an igloo or teepee for a year?

288 **WYR** blow your nose with sandpaper or use bubble wrap instead of toilet paper?

289 **WYR** ride a bucking bull in a rodeo or be the rodeo clown who distracts the bull for the rider?

290 **WYR** have more muscular arms or legs?

291 **WYR** have cars that fly or pots of gold at the end of every rainbow?

292 **WYR** date someone successful but mean or someone unemployed but sweet?

293 **WYR** be stuck in an elevator or on a Ferris wheel for 24 hours?

294 **WYR** have a good credit score or good reputation?

295 **WYR** know what heaven or hell looks like?

296 **WYR** save Mufasa from *The Lion King* or Bambi's mom from dying?

297 **WYR** find a dead body in your car or 50 live snakes?

298 **WYR** never pay another electric bill or cell phone bill again?

299 **WYR** have to outrun an active volcano erupting or outrun a tsunami making landfall?

300 **WYR** have a talking bird or dancing turtle as a pet?

301 **WYR** have your biography written or your journal published?

302 **WYR** eat uncooked rice or uncooked macaroni?

303 **WYR** have milk in your tea or coffee?

304 **WYR** erase your past or change it?

305 **WYR** have your lips permanently pursed or injected with too much filler?

306 **WYR** eat a cinnamon stick or bay leaf?

307 **WYR** your body or your face age?

308 **WYR** have red or brown freckles?

309 **WYR** eat dirt or weeds?

310 **WYR** lie in a bath of slime or dirty dish water?

311 **WYR** open your heart or protect it?

312 **WYR** date someone who will treat you right or who will spoil you?

313 **WYR** shop on Black Friday or the day after Christmas?

314 **WYR** see a dancing polar bear or a fox that can twirl?

315 **WYR** never wear black or white again?

316 **WYR** keep a first aid kit or weapon in your car?

317 **WYR** play doubles or singles in tennis?

318 **WYR** have a long-distance or online relationship?

319 **WYR** fall in love with someone you've known your whole life or just met?

320 **WYR** play solitaire or go fish?

321 **WYR** drive on the wrong side of the road or drive double the posted speed limit?

322 **WYR** clone your pet or a family member?

323 **WYR** projectile vomit or diarrhea?

324 **WYR** witness the sky falling or it raining men?

325 **WYR** be Type A or B personality?

326 **WYR** stand on an ant pile for 5 minutes or near a swarming beehive for an hour?

327 **WYR** spend the night in a dumpster or a porta-potty?

328 **WYR** your crush see you pick your nose or hear you fart?

329 **WYR** wear adult diapers the rest of your life or never wear underwear again?

330 **WYR** be an executioner on death row for a month or a crash test dummy for a day?

331 **WYR** hula hoop with your neck or leg?

332 **WYR** live in *The Blair Witch Project* or *Paranormal Activity*?

333 **WYR** lick a fire hydrant or a door handle for a busy store?

334 **WYR** have lobster claws or hedge clippers for hands?

335 **WYR** be in allegiance with Tony Soprano or Tony Montana?

336 **WYR** never be able to go to the beach again or live off grid for a year?

337 **WYR** be able to manipulate weather or speak to the dead?

338 **WYR** have your laugh sound like a hyena or a cow mooing?

339 **WYR** take credit for something you didn't do or blame someone for something you did bad?

340 **WYR** always judge others or always have others judge you?

341 **WYR** get bit by a vampire or a dog with rabies?

342 **WYR** compete in *Survivor* or *The Amazing Race*?

343 **WYR** get in the ring and fight Muhammed Ali or Floyd Mayweather?

344 **WYR** visit a chiropractor or acupuncturist when your back hurts?

345 **WYR** fly a kite in a rainstorm or walk barefoot on hot coals?

346 **WYR** eat the dangerous delicacy of pufferfish or sip absinthe?

347 **WYR** put ketchup or ranch dressing on everything you eat?

348 **WYR** never be able to have a bank account again or never be able to own a business?

349 **WYR** have magic shoes that make you invisible or magic glasses that incinerate things?

350 **WYR** your significant other cheat with your best friend or with your twin?

351 **WYR** live without smoke detectors or fire extinguishers?

352 **WYR** suck a stranger's thumb or pick your mom's nose?

353 **WYR** have a poodle or pug?

354 **WYR** see lemurs or aardvarks at your zoo?

355 **WYR** take a photo with Santa or the Easter bunny?

356 **WYR** live in denial or shame?

357 **WYR** play with Silly Putty or Play-Doh?

358 **WYR** have blurry vision or be colorblind?

359 **WYR** make amends or move on?

360 **WYR** microwave or stovetop popcorn?

361 **WYR** drink almond milk or soy milk?

362 **WYR** swim with dolphins or manatees?

363 **WYR** tour a wax museum or observatory?

364 **WYR** have a bubble bath or hot shower?

365 **WYR** eat honey mustard or thousand island dressing?

366 **WYR** your ears be too small or too big?

367 **WYR** wear a fedora or beret?

368 **WYR** build sandcastles or boogie board at the beach?

369 **WYR** play Simon or Memory?

370 **WYR** never get a headache or stomach ache again?

371 **WYR** sleep on a pillow top or memory foam mattress?

372 **WYR** play hangman or tic-tac-toe?

373 **WYR** be the first person to explore a planet or take an experimental drug?

374 **WYR** be near sided or far sided?

375 **WYR** head bang or slam dance?

376 **WYR** have Velcro hands or feet?

377 **WYR** sleep in a spooky attic or an eerie basement?

378 **WYR** have webbed hands or webbed feet?

379 **WYR** Godzilla or King Kong be real?

380 **WYR** wear a onesie 24/7 for a year or a horse head costume for a month straight?

381 **WYR** have suction cup like hands or wheels on your feet?

382 **WYR** have your own secret handshake or secret language?

383 **WYR** eat bacon flavored desserts or sweet flavored meats?

384 **WYR** play Chinese checkers or chess?

385 **WYR** encourage others or be generous?

386 **WYR** suck a worm flavored lollipop or lick snail flavored ice cream?

387 **WYR** have two left feet or your eyes in the back of your head?

388 **WYR** be a long-distance runner or sprinter?

389 **WYR** make webs like a spider or lift 1,000 times your weight like an ant?

390 **WYR** own a horse with wings like Pegasus or a talking dog with human intelligence?

391 **WYR** have James Bond's gadgets or Batman's toys?

392 **WYR** be an assassin or a spy?

393 **WYR** live on Twinkies and Spam or raw fish and moldy cheese for a year?

394 **WYR** your eyes have night vision capabilities or your ears have sonar capabilities?

395 **WYR** bring back Elvis or Michael Jackson?

396 **WYR** be superficial or superstitious?

397 **WYR** live in a cave behind a waterfall or in an underground cavern?

398 **WYR** date a person convicted of murder or a person convicted of running a Ponzi scam?

399 **WYR** have one glass eye or one robotic prosthetic arm?

400 **WYR** go on a Mediterranean cruise or an African safari?

401 **WYR** know how to use a blow dart or slingshot?

402 **WYR** be trapped under your ex's bed or in your parents' closet?

403 **WYR** eat earthworms or dung beetles?

404 **WYR** have an infestation of mice or flying cockroaches in your home?

405 **WYR** have the power to cast spells on people or cure the sick?

406 **WYR** die before or after your spouse?

407 **WYR** dine with royalty or geniuses?

408 **WYR** try and survive an avalanche or a mudslide?

409 **WYR** give up fried foods or sugar forever?

410 **WYR** have a funny tombstone or a heartfelt memorial resting place?

411 **WYR** rap onstage with Eminem or Jay-Z?

412 **WYR** use lotion that has bug guts in it or shampoo where the main ingredient is pig blood?

413 **WYR** have skin like a snake or teeth like a crocodile?

414 **WYR** have more hours in your day or an extra day in the week?

415 **WYR** never see another sunset or sunrise?

416 **WYR** burp every time you kiss someone or laugh loudly every time you meet a new person?

417 **WYR** live in a socialist or totalitarian society?

418 **WYR** be seated on a plane next to a screaming baby or someone with bad body odor?

419 **WYR** have Albert Einstein as a teacher or Stephen Hawking as a mentor?

420 **WYR** collaborate on a book with Stephen King or J.K. Rowling?

421 **WYR** face the Grim Reaper or Freddy Krueger?

422 **WYR** have to read everything in braille or script that you have to decode?

423 **WYR** enter a secret portal to an alternate universe or secret door to the afterlife?

424 **WYR** trek through a snow-covered wilderness or desolate desert?

425 **WYR** be a private detective or gossip columnist?

426 **WYR** be on the cover of *People* or *TIME* magazine?

427 **WYR** play Spin the Bottle or truth or dare every day?

428 **WYR** live in a cabin deep in the swamp or a tree house in the jungle?

429 **WYR** be an experimental patient for cryogenics or for human cloning?

430 **WYR** munch on trail mix or granola bars when you're hiking?

431 **WYR** soak in a hot spring or float down a lazy river?

432 **WYR** use a canteen or a thermos?

433 **WYR** wear low tops or high tops?

434 **WYR** do crosswords or word search puzzles?

435 **WYR** play Yahtzee or Scrabble?

436 **WYR** find a kindred spirit or soulmate?

437 **WYR** have a trundle bed or pullout sofa bed?

438 **WYR** ration your food or water in the event of an emergency?

439 **WYR** have a telescope or microscope?

440 **WYR** fight an octopus or squid underwater?

441 **WYR** be intrusive or obtuse?

442 **WYR** collect bottle tops or trading cards?

443 **WYR** snuggle a sloth or kiss a koala?

444 **WYR** do tricks with a hacky sack or yo-yo?

445 **WYR** be able to balance on your head or fingertip?

446 **WYR** join the Army reserves or the Coast Guard reserves?

447 **WYR** play the fiddle or cello?

448 **WYR** be able to change a person's mood or mind?

449 **WYR** your home smell like fresh baked bread or fresh baked cookies?

450 **WYR** assemble model trains or planes?

451 **WYR** listen to a lullaby or nursery rhymes?

452 **WYR** get a haircut from a toddler or have your thumbnails pulled off by pliers?

453 **WYR** have team spirit or good sportsmanship?

454 **WYR** tape your eyes open or your nose back?

455 **WYR** defend yourself with a hockey stick or baseball bat?

456 **WYR** eat a small can of dog food or a bowl of cereal with spoiled milk?

457 **WYR** be covered in flies or maggots?

458 **WYR** tour a slaughterhouse where animals die or sit in on an execution?

459 **WYR** your best friend break a promise or your significant other lie to you?

460 **WYR** have a poem or a song written about you?

461 **WYR** have your life pattern a *Choose Your Own Adventure* book or a cheesy romance novel?

462 **WYR** plant trees or clean up trash on the side of the roads for Earth Day?

463 **WYR** have eyes like a frog or a tongue like a snake?

464 **WYR** have an adventure like Red Riding Hood or Goldie Locks?

465 **WYR** have neighbors that party all the time or ones that snoop and spy on you?

466 **WYR** get your heart broken but learn a lesson or break someone's heart and feel guilty?

467 **WYR** go into business with family or someone you respect?

468 **WYR** be trained in martial arts or boxing?

469 **WYR** have a bad case of agoraphobia or photophobia?

470 **WYR** live a short life but die a hero or live a long time but people think you're a coward?

471 **WYR** date a psychopath or sociopath?

472 **WYR** have a physical disfiguration or a mental illness?

473 **WYR** have breakfast for dinner or pizza for breakfast every day for a year?

474 **WYR** eat pigs' feet or chicken feet?

475 **WYR** go without electricity or running water for a week?

476 **WYR** attend a celebrity séance or a book reading with your favorite author?

477 **WYR** eat 5 of the hottest peppers in the world or a stew made with crickets and grubworms?

478 **WYR** find a new species or a new planet?

479 **WYR** get caught internet stalking your ex or accidentally send a nude pic to your mom?

480 **WYR** know all your parent's secrets or all the skeletons in your significant other's closet?

481 **WYR** be roasted by comedian Kevin Hart or Sarah Silverman?

482 **WYR** live in an area where there are lots of tornadoes or earthquakes?

483 **WYR** apologize more or argue less?

484 **WYR** eat soggy vegetables or stale chips?

485 **WYR** deep dish or thin crust pizza?

486 **WYR** crush a snail shell with your teeth or scale a fish with your fingernails?

487 **WYR** always eat dessert first or skip dessert?

488 **WYR** wear shackles or a strait jacket for 48 hours?

489 **WYR** clean 10 dirty toilets or wash 5 piles of dirty dishes?

490 **WYR** read a book or listen to an audio book?

491 **WYR** watch football or the Macy's parade on Thanksgiving?

492 **WYR** have gnats in your drink or a fly in your food?

493 **WYR** have Frosted Flakes or Raisin Bran?

494 **WYR** be lactose intolerant or have a gluten allergy?

495 **WRY** play pool or bowling?

496 **WYR** have strobe lights or a disco ball at your next party?

497 **WYR** get a broken eye socket or broken jaw?

498 **WYR** have IHOP or Waffle House?

499 **WYR** have your mom's cooking or your grandma's cooking?

500 **WYR** have long stem roses or tulips?

501 **WYR** have the *Prom Night* or *Carrie* experience?

502 **WYR** try to crack a coconut or a safe?

503 **WYR** have Wheat Thins or Triscuits?

504 **WYR** always know what you're getting for Christmas or be surprised?

505 **WYR** manage your emotions or manage your stress level?

506 **WYR** have an umbrella or rain boots in a downpour?

507 **WYR** cross paths with a wicked scarecrow or sinister raven?

508 **WYR** sleepwalk for a year or be in a coma for a month?

509 **WYR** never be able to use GPS ever or never take another elevator again?

510 **WYR** star in one season of a reality TV show or be an extra in at least 50 movies?

511 **WYR** meet Leonardo da Vinci or Mother Teresa?

512 **WYR** have unlimited storage space on your smart phone or laptop?

513 **WYR** your mom or your boss get a copy of every text you get?

514 **WYR** get dentures or wear braces on your teeth the rest of your life?

515 **WYR** look at the browser history of your significant other or your boss?

516 **WYR** change your first name to a name you hate or get a small tattoo on your face?

517 **WYR** be locked in a room with someone you hate or Pennywise the clown?

518 **WYR** have a pet porcupine or pet skunk?

519 **WYR** be kidnapped by your ex or your current significant other's ex?

520 **WYR** contract a condition like Benjamin Button or live with leprosy?

521 **WYR** learn dancing from Channing Tatum or Jabbawockeez?

522 **WYR** be stuck inside *Mario Bros World* or the *Grand Theft Auto* video game?

523 **WYR** have a photographic memory or heightened senses?

524 **WYR** go trick-or-treating with Leatherface or Jason Voorhees?

525 **WYR** have to grow, hunt and kill your own food or eat only Taco Bell for a year?

526 **WYR** only bathe in rainwater or never use deodorant?

527 **WYR** stay in a different hotel each night for a year or have to be home by midnight forever?

528 **WYR** lose your ability to fall in love or your ability to discern right and wrong?

529 **WYR** have a secret admirer or be a secret admirer?

530 **WYR** have to wear a shirt every day that says, "I farted" or "I'm with Stupid?"

531 **WYR** swim in a tank full of piranhas or electric eels?

532 **WYR** your children or significant other be punished for the mistakes you make?

533 **WYR** be sucked into a virtual reality or live on the moon?

534 **WYR** have long nose hair or long ear hair?

535 **WYR** never wear shoes or underwear?

536 **WYR** talk your way out of a fight or fight your way out of a kidnapping?

537 **WYR** lick every inanimate object you see or be licked by every living thing you see?

538 **WYR** be able to eat food that's only free or drink only rainwater?

539 **WYR** kiss a dog that just licked themselves or a cat that just ate a rat?

540 **WYR** work as a urologist or a crime scene cleaner?

541 **WYR** milk a cow or milk a snake?

542 **WYR** forget how to speak or walk?

543 **WYR** run in a human hamster wheel or poop in a human litter box?

544 **WYR** take a window seat or aisle seat on a plane?

545 **WYR** crack your knuckles or pop your back?

546 **WYR** have your own bouncy house or waterslide?

547 **WYR** forget how to spell or add?

548 **WYR** be able to move objects with your mind or make them disappear with a clap?

549 **WYR** eat Tic Tacs or Mentos?

550 **WYR** have skin like a cactus or pineapple?

551 **WYR** jump in a pile of leaves or snow?

552 **WYR** lick the puss out of a popped zit or busted blister?

553 **WYR** sleep with only a sheet or only a blanket?

554 **WYR** blow up 100 balloons or lick 500 envelopes?

555 **WYR** faint when you see blood or scream when you see your reflection in a mirror?

556 **WYR** be an average person now or a king/queen living centuries ago?

557 **WYR** have giraffe legs or flamingo legs?

558 **WYR** smell fresh laundry or fresh cut grass?

559 **WYR** eat a banana peel or bird feather?

560 **WYR** get divorced 3 times or never get married?

561 **WYR** have an affair with an influential politician or a powerful attorney?

562 **WYR** play one on one basketball with Michael Jordan or Kobe Bryant?

563 **WYR** have high tea with Sharon Osbourne or the Queen of England?

564 **WYR** go a year missing your two front teeth or talk with a bad lisp forever?

565 **WYR** attend a Halloween party hosted by mad scientists or cannibals?

566 **WYR** drive a VW bug painted every color of the rainbow or dress like the 70s era for a year?

567 **WYR** have a significant other that's too flirty or one who complains too much?

568 **WYR** get compliments on your intelligence or looks?

569 **WYR** have your own jetpack or get the chance to travel at the speed of light?

570 **WYR** cry tears of blood or have a cold the rest of your life?

571 **WYR** allow your body to host an alien species until it's born or live with parasites forever?

572 **WYR** make one person's dreams come true or buy lunch for 10 starving kids?

573 **WYR** have a *50 Shades of Grey* romance or a *Pretty Woman* love story?

574 **WYR** live among the clouds or beneath the ocean?

575 **WYR** have your head be too big for your body or hands that are too small for your size?

576 **WYR** have hair on your back or go completely bald?

577 **WYR** have your house smell like a skunk or rotting trash?

578 **WYR** walk on scorpion infested land or swim through jellyfish infested water?

579 **WYR** eat a taco made of bugs or weird animal parts?

580 **WYR** lick the bottom of your shoes or your toilet seat?

581 **WYR** be great at sports or at trivia?

582 **WYR** live under a bridge or in a condemned building?

583 **WYR** get too little sleep or too little to eat daily?

584 **WYR** drink dirty dishwater or your own puke?

585 **WYR** your country goes to war again or battle a plague outbreak?

586 **WYR** have looks that could kill or a killer look?

587 **WYR** avoid stupid people or annoying people?

588 **WYR** be braver or stronger?

589 **WYR** fix two of your friends up together or stay out of their love life?

590 **WYR** let sleeping dogs lie or let the cat out of the bag?

591 **WYR** steal someone's thunder or give them a taste of their own medicine?

592 **WYR** lie on your resume or a job application?

593 **WYR** get body slammed by a pro wrestler or kicked by an MMA fighter?

594 **WYR** eat celery with pimento cheese or carrot sticks with dip?

595 **WYR** be considerate or cunning?

596 **WYR** attend a bonfire or wine tasting?

597 **WYR** forget to wear deodorant or brush your teeth before your date?

598 **WYR** sleep all weekend or be out and about all weekend?

599 **WYR** be a referee or coach?

600 **WYR** have too many allergies or too many phobias?

601 **WYR** wrap everything you eat in bacon or slather it with butter?

602 **WYR** others hear your thoughts or see what's in your head?

603 **WYR** sleep on a waterbed or bunk bed?

604 **WYR** be a drill sergeant or run a boot camp?

605 **WYR** break up a fight or record it and post it to YouTube?

606 **WYR** be all knowing or all seeing?

607 **WYR** always leave the party early or always be the last to leave?

608 **WYR** make more money or do more meaningful work?

609 **WYR** live in a house with no roof or no windows?

610 **WYR** use a dirty sock or your hand as toilet paper?

611 **WYR** count the stars in the sky or all the leaves on a tree?

612 **WYR** have children when you're too young or too old?

613 **WYR** snoop through your enemy's phone or snoop around their home?

614 **WYR** spend the night at the White House or Buckingham Palace?

615 **WYR** eat coffee flavored everything or put jelly beans on everything you eat for a year?

616 **WYR** wear a bathing suit to a formal event or wear ugly formal clothes to a party?

617 **WYR** borrow money from a loan shark or the biggest gossip you know?

618 **WYR** explore the Grand Canyon in the dark or the Amazon Rainforest during a rain storm?

619 **WYR** test drive the world's fastest car or the world's most luxurious car?

620 **WYR** tour the food scene in Paris or Italy?

621 **WYR** be frozen at your current age forever or give your parents 10 extra years of life?

622 **WYR** be able to run super-fast or have the strength of 10 humans?

623 **WYR** experiment with voodoo or fortune telling?

624 **WYR** have your own private island or your own airline?

625 **WYR** have a mullet or super long dreads?

626 **WYR** solve the Jack the Ripper murder or solve the Zodiac murders?

627 **WYR** not have any friends or have friends that you don't trust?

628 **WYR** live in a home made of tin cans or popsicle sticks?

629 **WYR** never be able to use a credit card again or pay for food only using pennies?

630 **WYR** have Jurassic Park be real or have more Disney Worlds be built?

631 **WYR** battle Moby Dick or Jaws?

632 **WYR** have no eyebrows or an extra finger?

633 **WYR** watch 365 days of horror movies or rom coms?

634 **WYR** have a child that was a bully or very rebellious?

635 **WYR** have a job that you're over qualified for or under qualified for?

636 **WYR** be a journalist for *Rolling Stone* or *New York Times*?

637 **WYR** be Captain of the Death Star or Enterprise?

638 **WYR** jump to conclusions or make assumptions?

639 **WYR** feed a mouse to a snake or a bird to a cat?

640 **WYR** lick a bone your dog's been chewing on or wipe your car windshield with your cheek?

641 **WYR** have eagle talons or vampire fangs?

642 **WYR** battle pirates or vikings?

643 **WYR** rescue baby turtles or baby otters?

644 **WYR** your kids take the bus to school or you drive them?

645 **WYR** ride the scariest waterslide or tallest ride at an amusement park?

646 **WYR** get locked out of your house or your car?

647 **WYR** your fingers always feel sticky or your throat always feel itchy?

648 **WYR** your feet always feel on fire or frozen?

649 **WYR** BASE jump or jump out of an airplane over water with no parachute?

650 **WYR** believe in ghosts or aliens?

651 **WYR** live with no regrets or live carefree?

652 **WYR** listen to the same song 24-hours on repeat or watch the same movie for a week?

653 **WYR** have more charm or more character?

654 **WYR** build a fort out of nature or sheets?

655 **WYR** your heels or palms itch?

656 **WYR** have a hairy back or hairy stomach?

657 **WYR** eat a fly or moth?

658 **WYR** be a friendly ghost or a vengeful phantom when you die?

659 **WYR** drink a slug shake or leech smoothie?

660 **WYR** eat Hot Tamales the candy or actual tamales?

661 **WYR** listen to someone's confession or problems?

662 **WYR** play the banjo or tambourine?

663 **WYR** break dance every time you hear a car horn or twerk every time you hear birds chirp?

664 **WYR** lie to a priest or lie under oath?

665 **WYR** die before the world ends or die watching the world come to an end?

666 **WYR** pick your lotto numbers from your fortune cookie or from your horoscope?

667 **WYR** be kicked in the head by a mule or hit in the head by a foul ball at a baseball game?

668 **WYR** suffer from paranoia or be very superstitious to the point of crazy?

669 **WYR** learn ballroom dancing or hip-hop dancing?

670 **WYR** eat BBQ road kill or opossum stew?

671 **WYR** always have peace in your relationships or always win every argument you're in?

672 **WYR** wear cowboy boots every day for a month or ballet slippers for a week?

673 **WYR** abolish animal testing forever or make humans go through the same tests animals do?

674 **WYR** be able to talk to angels or see demons around you?

675 **WYR** attempt to swallow a sword or fire?

676 **WYR** free all the innocent people in jail or lock up all the criminals still out on the street?

677 **WYR** hang around rude people who were honest or nice people who were completely fake?

678 **WYR** make up for lost time with someone or erase a painful memory?

679 **WYR** humiliate your significant other or your parents?

680 **WYR** be too overweight or too anorexic?

681 **WYR** creep everyone out you meet or be creeped out by everyone you meet?

682 **WYR** go spelunking or try hardcore parkour?

683 **WYR** drive in a NASCAR race or be a jockey at the Kentucky Derby?

684 **WYR** be trapped in a runaway train or a falling elevator?

685 **WYR** visit a sex shop with your grandmother or spend a month in a convent?

686 **WYR** zipline through fire or run through quicksand?

687 **WYR** only be allowed to watch animated movies or only black and white movies?

688 **WYR** be a victim of catfish or be the one catfishing a person?

689 **WYR** sacrifice your integrity or pride for someone you love?

690 **WYR** have corn on the cobb or off the cobb?

691 **WYR** live in the moment or obsess about the future?

692 **WYR** find a dinosaur egg or lost treasure from the Ming Dynasty?

693 **WYR** everyone think you're fake or think you're shallow?

694 **WYR** go ice fishing or deep-sea fishing?

695 **WYR** write with your eyes closed or with your nondominant hand?

696 **WYR** race wheel chairs or motorized chairs?

697 **WYR** eat glue or pencil erasers?

698 **WYR** look through the gym locker of someone you find hot or have them spot you a set?

799 **WYR** get your hand stuck in a meat grinder or blender?

700 **WYR** have endless adrenaline rushes or endless access to knowledge?

701 **WYR** dress to impress or dress for success?

702 **WYR** get poison ivy in your ear or in your nose?

703 **WYR** always spit or drool when you talk?

704 **WYR** always be thankful or mindful?

705 **WYR** have your spouse or your child be ashamed of you?

706 **WYR** be candid or cutthroat?

707 **WYR** have your hairline move back two inches or all your teeth be discolored?

708 **WYR** have something invisible attacking your funny bone or your eardrum?

709 **WYR** accidentally laugh loudly at a funeral or fart while giving a speech at a wedding?

710 **WYR** live in a humid or dry climate?

711 **WYR** have ear wax as big as corn flakes or boogers as big as Cheerios?

712 **WYR** split your lip or stub your toe?

713 **WYR** bite your tongue or always speak what's on your mind?

714 **WYR** always have an itch you can't scratch or have a thirst you can't quench?

715 **WYR** always feel bloated but can't burp or always feel like sneezing but never sneeze?

716 **WYR** ride in a self-driving car you can't control or drive the smallest car in the world for free?

717 **WYR** suffer from a tooth ache or ear ache all day?

718 **WYR** people envy you or admire you?

719 **WYR** be the victim of a carjacking or identity theft?

720 **WYR** have money problems or health issues?

721 **WYR** inherit money or property?

722 **WYR** discover the unknown or explore the familiar?

723 **WYR** have a flower of the month or dessert of the month subscription?

724 **WYR** eat salads or drink smoothies every day for a week?

725 **WYR** eliminate AIDS or influenza from the planet?

726 **WYR** donate a kidney or bone marrow?

727 **WYR** have more patience or motivation?

728 **WYR** lose all the photos you've ever taken on your smart phone or have your identity stolen?

729 **WYR** the world had one government that is all a democracy or everything stay as it is now?

730 **WYR** be in a Taylor Swift or Beyoncé music video?

731 **WYR** get premature gray hair or have terrible ear hair?

732 **WYR** enter a badminton or ping pong tournament for a chance to win money?

733 **WYR** be inside an Alfred Hitchcock movie thriller or an Agatha Christie short story mystery?

734 **WYR** attend group therapy for support or have one on one counselling for privacy?

735 **WYR** own an experimental robot dog or experimental drug for heightened intelligence?

736 **WYR** have a career as an ATF agent or U.S. Marshal?

737 **WYR** be the most trusted sidekick of Billy the Kid or Al Capone?

738 **WYR** have an EPIC bachelor/bachelorette party and average wedding or vice versa?

739 **WYR** buy a radio network or a publishing house?

740 **WYR** go back in time and prevent Chernobyl or the Holocaust?

741 **WYR** cuddle a koala bear or baby panda bear?

742 **WYR** have an appealing swagger or a style people try to copy?

743 **WYR** have a real live Winnie the Pooh or Paddington Bear?

744 **WYR** be controversial or unpopular?

745 **WYR** never use Snapchat or Periscope ever again?

746 **WYR** eat toilet paper or notebook paper?

747 **WYR** accidentally walk into a snake pit or wasps' nest?

748 **WYR** drink water with a dead rat in it or drink your own urine when you're dehydrated?

749 **WYR** walk like a runway model or John Travolta's character Tony Manero?

750 **WYR** have a mustache that can never be shaved or an extra tongue?

751 **WYR** fall asleep during your wedding ceremony or get lost on your honeymoon?

752 **WYR** be a hostage negotiator or talk a jumper down off a ledge?

753 **WYR** have Donald Trump's hair or Jay Leno's chin?

754 **WYR** your voice sound like Gilbert Gottfried or Fran Drescher?

755 **WYR** decorate a gingerbread house or make gingerbread cookies?

756 **WYR** slip and fall in public or have a bad public breakup?

757 **WYR** drink beer from a bottle or frosted mug?

758 **WYR** your dandruff look like granola or acne look like bacon bits?

759 **WYR** laugh like a howler monkey or hyena?

760 **WYR** your job offers a naptime or recess?

761 **WYR** be forced to work on the first computer or use the first cellphone ever made?

762 **WYR** have ugly artwork on your walls or no artwork at all?

763 **WYR** hear or move like a 90-year-old senior?

764 **WYR** give yourself a facial with a toilet brush or foot pumice stone?

765 **WYR** drink prune juice or tomato juice?

766 **WYR** choose your career or a family?

767 **WYR** smell like bleach or Listerine?

768 **WYR** be a doctor for a famous sports team or a small village in Africa?

769 **WYR** live without air conditioning or hot water?

770 **WYR** go back and get to do high school all over again or have all your debt paid off?

771 **WYR** date someone you met online or someone your parents set you up with?

772 **WYR** have more time for yourself or more sleep each day?

773 **WYR** eat food out of a trash can or eat food with mold all over it?

774 **WYR** find a fingernail or worm in your salad?

775 **WYR** get stung by a group of scorpions or stand on a fire ant mound for 10 minutes?

776 **WYR** be a conjoined twin or be born with polymelia?

777 **WYR** be interviewed by Barbara Walters or Howard Stern?

778 **WYR** be serenaded by Celine Dion or Barbra Streisand?

779 **WYR** go on a dating game show or online dating site to find love?

780 **WYR** the voice of your conscience sound like Bugs Bunny or Robert De Niro?

781 **WYR** be more creative or more intuitive?

782 **WYR** learn how to send and decode Morse code or learn how to read braille?

783 **WYR** only have one friend the rest of your life or never be able to get divorced?

784 **WYR** have your own stylist and personal tailor or eat at any restaurant for free whenever?

785 **WYR** be served breakfast in bed daily or get an extra hour sleep daily?

786 **WYR** write greeting cards or obituaries for a living?

787 **WYR** consult an Ouija Board or Magic 8 Ball for answers to your questions?

788 **WYR** box a kangaroo or tussle with a moose?

789 **WYR** eat your favorite food covered in roly-polies or tree bark?

790 **WYR** rock a combover hairstyle or dress like Alice Cooper?

791 **WYR** find a four-leaf clover or a really old penny?

792 **WYR** start a rumor or spread gossip you overheard?

793 **WYR** eat a 10-year-old fruitcake still in its package or drink expired eggnog?

794 **WYR** be protected from evil spirits or evil people?

795 **WYR** drive a 4-wheeler or dirt bike for fun?

796 **WYR** eat saltines or Ritz crackers?

797 **WYR** egg your least favorite teacher's car or someone who picked on you's head?

798 **WYR** stay at the Overlook Hotel or the Bates Motel?

799 **WYR** get an infected cut or ingrown toenail?

800 **WYR** be a fake psychic or sinister fortune teller?

801 **WYR** watch baby owls or baby penguins?

802 **WYR** be afraid to try new things or be so open minded that you never say no?

803 **WYR** skinny dip in the ocean or a neighborhood pool at night?

804 **WYR** wear V-neck or crew tees?

805 **WYR** always kill two birds with one stone or handle things one at a time?

806 **WYR** look for the silver lining or just go to sleep and wait for the day to be over?

807 **WYR** have a white Christmas or a tropical Christmas?

808 **WYR** have a pebble in your shoe or an eyelash in your eye you can never get out?

809 **WYR** stomp the yard or get into the groove?

810 **WYR** be a charmer or puppet master?

811 **WYR** be a dentist or podiatrist?

812 **WYR** get burned by a hot curling iron or boiling water?

813 **WYR** your eyebrows or arm hair come to life and dance every full moon?

814 **WYR** always maintain control or maintain order?

815 **WYR** seek the truth or pursue your dreams?

816 **WYR** have hammer toes or clubbed thumbs?

817 **WYR** dye your hair or shave in a public restroom?

818 **WYR** people be less obsessed with money or sex?

819 **WYR** only buy hybrid cars or never buy a hybrid?

820 **WYR** eat a spoonful of wasabi or one ghost pepper?

821 **WYR** own Darth Vader's helmet or Michael Jackson's "Thriller" jacket?

822 **WYR** attempt the cinnamon challenge or the saltine challenge?

823 **WYR** try and do a handstand while surfing or waterski with no skis?

824 **WYR** live life with "no regrets" or "no what-ifs?"

825 **WYR** try snake charming or get hypnotized?

826 **WYR** experience 40 days of rain or 40 days of darkness without sun?

827 **WYR** have a summer romance or spring fling?

828 **WYR** the disco era or flapper era come back around?

829 **WYR** walk through a river filled with leeches or snapping turtles?

830 **WYR** be trapped in a room with bats or rats?

831 **WYR** have a road trip with Donald Trump or O.J. Simpson?

832 **WYR** have a roommate who was quiet and asocial or loud and obnoxious?

833 **WYR** open your front door and see Jigsaw or Michael Myers?

834 **WYR** eat whole coffee beans or lemon seeds?

835 **WYR** lose your keys down a sewer drain or down an elevator shaft?

836 **WYR** sleep on a bed of rose thorns or bed of hay animals have slept on?

837 **WYR** always get the latest smartphone for free or get free haircuts the rest of your life?

838 **WYR** live in a bright pink house or a house where the grass is never mowed?

839 **WYR** spend the night in Alcatraz or on the Island of the Dolls in Mexico?

840 **WYR** compete on *American Idol* or *The Voice*?

841 **WYR** be able to count your blessings or your money?

842 **WYR** enter a hot dog or a pie eating contest?

843 **WYR** be a good fighter or good lover?

844 **WYR** drink the best coffee in the world or sample the finest chocolate ever made?

845 **WYR** have perfect teeth or perfect hair?

846 **WYR** see one of your parents having an affair or see your spouse having an affair?

847 **WYR** be the brunt of a joke or have people think you're a joke?

848 **WYR** be seen as an antagonist or protagonist?

849 **WYR** watch sci-fi or animated movies?

850 **WYR** eat chowder or chili?

851 **WYR** eat onion rings or onion strings?

852 **WYR** wear flannel or thermals in the winter?

853 **WYR** have a lighter load or an easier schedule?

854 **WYR** have tortilla chips with salsa or queso?

855 **WYR** be a drum major or cheerleader?

856 **WYR** nibble on fresh mozzarella or parmesan cheese?

857 **WYR** feel empowered or elated?

858 **WYR** use a dating app or a dating service?

859 **WYR** people prejudge you or criticize you?

860 **WYR** be featured on *America's Most Wanted* or the side of a milk carton by accident?

861 **WYR** be hands on or hands off when it comes to raising kids?

862 **WYR** play water polo or traditional polo?

863 **WYR** give someone flowers or a fruit basket for a gift?

864 **WYR** star in the musical *Grease* or *Wicked*?

865 **WYR** be a thrill seeker or truth seeker?

866 **WYR** be someone's hero or role model?

867 **WYR** aliens look like the ones from *E.T. the Extra-Terrestrial* or *Independence Day*?

868 **WYR** the planet has less pollution or less population?

869 **WYR** be obsessed with taking and posting selfies to social media or have full-blown OCD?

870 **WYR** live next door to a cemetery or snake farm?

871 **WYR** become a brain surgeon or heart surgeon?

872 **WYR** accidentally break your arm or accidentally break your friend's arm?

873 **WYR** explore Suicide Forest in Japan or the Gomantong Caves in Malaysia?

874 **WYR** look for a needle in a haystack or put together a 40,000-piece puzzle?

875 **WYR** get a fish pedicure or caviar facial?

876 **WYR** inherit a vineyard or a farm?

877 **WYR** try volcano boarding at Cerro Negro or kayak down Niagara Falls?

878 **WYR** participate in the Running of the Bulls in Spain or get in the Cage of Death in Australia?

879 **WYR** spend the night in the Taj Mahal or the Vatican?

880 **WYR** help release baby turtles back into the ocean or volunteer at an elephant sanctuary?

881 **WYR** set a Guinness World Record or visit the North Pole?

882 **WYR** drive a military tank or fly in a fighter jet?

883 **WYR** take your friends up in a hot air balloon or host a dinner in the sky party?

884 **WYR** drive the entire Route 66 or walk the Great Wall of China?

885 **WYR** play with the Trans-Siberian Orchestra or the New York Philharmonic?

886 **WYR** be good at 10 things or master one thing with excellence?

887 **WYR** never wear tennis shoes or underwear again?

888 **WYR** go to a job interview with really bad dandruff or bad breath?

889 **WYR** feel like you're slowly going insane or like you're losing your muscle strength?

890 **WYR** be a door to door salesperson or sell used cars?

891 **WYR** live in a world where plants can eat humans or birds attack humans?

892 **WYR** find a rare artifact or find a forgotten time capsule from 50 years ago?

893 **WYR** crack down harder on people texting and driving or drinking and driving?

894 **WYR** write a book about a subject you hate or write a song for a singer you dislike?

895 **WYR** have someone shoot an apple off your head via arrow or throwing knife?

896 **WYR** be a widow or divorcee?

897 **WYR** know the outcome of the choices you make in advance or leave everything to chance?

898 **WYR** jam with Lenny Kravitz or Jimi Hendrix?

899 **WYR** people dress age appropriate or however they want?

900 **WYR** heckle a bad comedian or roast an annoying co-worker?

901 **WYR** be a team leader or a team player?

902 **WYR** battle Lyme disease or Lupus?

903 **WYR** join a cult or start your own religion?

904 **WYR** get road rash from a fall or tangled in a barbed wire fence?

905 **WYR** have a teacup pig or mini horse?

906 **WYR** realize a blessing in disguise or have your cake and eat it too?

907 **WYR** have a ceiling fan or oscillating fan?

908 **WYR** be the devil's advocate or just be the devil on someone's shoulder?

909 **WYR** sculpt ice or clay?

910 **WYR** help a friend break out of jail or get out of a bad relationship?

911 **WYR** eat a raw clove of garlic or a raw onion?

912 **WYR** use your car's a/c or drive with the windows down?

913 **WYR** work in a school or prison cafeteria?

914 **WYR** attend a focus group or mock jury and get paid?

915 **WYR** be the bearer of bad news or be the shoulder to cry on?

916 **WYR** hear your soul speak or your heart sing?

917 **WYR** disappoint your parents or your grandparents?

918 **WYR** commit treason or espionage?

919 **WYR** be less possessive or fight for someone you love?

920 **WYR** say "I told you so" or "I love you?"

921 **WYR** feel like you're floating or sinking?

922 **WYR** drink flavored coffee or regular coffee?

923 **WYR** confront your accuser or confront your demons?

924 **WYR** eat bat guano or rat droppings?

925 **WYR** play *Family Feud* with your family or go on *Fear Factor* with your BFF?

926 **WYR** have a sensitivity to light or sound?

927 **WYR** have to memorize the dictionary or The Holy Bible?

928 **WYR** have a squirrel tail or chicken feathers on your arm?

929 **WYR** have more people at your wedding or funeral?

930 **WYR** age visibly more rapidly but live longer or age very slowly but die younger?

931 **WYR** have 365 days of snow or unrelenting drought like heat?

932 **WYR** snore loudly or talk in your sleep about secrets?

933 **WYR** be a target of a hitman or your family be victims of ransom?

934 **WYR** only ride public transportation or only be able to Uber for 1 year?

935 **WYR** be missing a thumb or have your right leg an inch shorter than the left?

936 **WYR** have an annoying voice or googly eyes?

937 **WYR** change your past or shape your future?

938 **WYR** play a card game of Poker or Go Fish, where your life depended on it?

939 **WYR** participate in a dangerous college hazing or anonymously turn in your fraternity?

940 **WYR** feel sleepy or hot all throughout your day?

941 **WYR** meet someone who enchanted you or who made you curious about the world?

942 **WYR** send a Voodoo doll or a horse head to your enemy?

943 **WYR** have a circus act as a trapeze artist or lion tamer?

944 **WYR** send more cyber bullies or cyber stalkers to jail?

945 **WYR** take part in an experimental transplant or uncertain holistic remedies?

946 **WYR** walk using orthopedic shoes or a cane?

947 **WYR** learn from every mistake or never make another mistake?

948 **WYR** throw up before each meal or burp for 30 minutes after each meal?

949 **WYR** be a badass or a superstar?

950 **WYR** make your dying confession to your significant other or best friend?

951 **WYR** talk about it or be about it?

952 **WYR** your car smell like spoiled milk or a stinky burp?

953 **WYR** have a hot shower or a hot meal?

954 **WYR** carpool to work or ride the bus?

955 **WYR** sip cappuccino or espresso?

956 **WYR** have someone steal one of your ideas or steal your significant other?

957 **WYR** learn from past mistakes or other's mistakes?

958 **WYR** run outside or run on a treadmill?

959 **WYR** snorkel or deep-sea dive?

960 **WYR** eat spinach or broccoli?

961 **WYR** feel haunted or cursed?

962 **WYR** drink sweet tea or black coffee?

963 **WYR** travel through time or space?

964 **WYR** eat double stuffed or regular Oreos?

965 **WYR** have a long neck or a long face?

966 **WYR** attend a masquerade ball or formal party?

967 **WYR** take the high road or get even?

968 **WYR** kill them with kindness or add insult to injury?

969 **WYR** wear cardigans or sweater vests?

970 **WYR** eat steak tartar or sashimi?

971 **WYR** have a penny for your thoughts or keep your thoughts to yourself?

972 **WYR** eat an expired can of tuna or a fresh can of cat food?

973 **WYR** feel obsolete or oppressed?

974 **WYR** suffer a head or back injury?

975 **WYR** have deep roots or deep insight?

976 **WYR** eat sardine ice cream or rat droppings?

977 **WYR** keep going back to the drawing board or change course?

978 **WYR** cross a river full of crocodiles or piranhas?

979 **WYR** see all the wonders of the world or meet 10 inspiring people before you die?

980 **WYR** steal a cop car or a firetruck?

981 **WYR** have a scary dentist or a creepy doctor?

982 **WYR** have mind control over a person or be able to manipulate time?

983 **WYR** lend a hand or lend money?

984 **WYR** have an endless supply of batteries or toilet paper?

985 **WYR** have a serious fear of the dark or an exaggerated fear of heights?

986 **WYR** convert to your fiancé's religion or have them convert to yours?

987 **WYR** join a cult or a biker gang?

988 **WYR** kiss someone with a tongue ring or braces?

989 **WYR** live on the most gorgeous beach in a tent or live on a lake in a boathouse?

990 **WYR** have an aggressive and dominant spouse or one who is meek and timid?

991 **WYR** have bad acne your whole life or go deaf in one ear?

992 **WYR** be a character in the last movie you saw or the last book you read?

993 **WYR** think too much or think too little?

994 **WYR** wear all black every day for a year or stay home every weekend for a year?

995 **WYR** try and save your house from a flood or fire?

996 **WYR** help a friend get off drugs or help a family member through a breakup?

997 **WYR** boycott the government or a big company for better working conditions?

998 **WYR** give up on falling in love or give up on a loved one who has gone astray?

999 **WYR** other people be more compassionate or more forgiving?

1000 **WYR** have a stalker like *Swimfan* or *Fatal Attraction*?

1001 **WYR** live in fear or live in debt?

1002 **WYR** have ugly friends or friends that were gorgeous?

1003 **WYR** be stuck in a horrible traffic jam or be present when a riot breaks out?

1004 **WYR** be part of an exorcism or spiritual cleansing?

1005 **WYR** spend the day surfing in the ocean or surfing the web?

1006 **WYR** be single for the next 10 years or attend 20 weddings in a row without a date?

1007 **WYR** have the Statue of Liberty or Mt. Rushmore come to life?

1008 **WYR** trek the Sahara Desert or Frozen Tundra?

1009 **WYR** design ugly Christmas sweaters or ugly neck ties?

1010 **WYR** be a 911 operator or an ambulance driver?

1011 **WYR** put your foot in your mouth when you speak or never speak?

1012 **WYR** have a surreal moment or an epiphany?

1013 **WYR** have a lavender or rosemary garden?

1014 **WYR** be Liberal or Conservative?

1015 **WYR** be a prisoner in your mind or a slave to love?

1016 **WYR** use PayPal or Apple Pay?

1017 **WYR** have a funny or tasteful tombstone?

1018 **WYR** eat frozen grapes or frozen yogurt?

1019 **WYR** have unlimited cheats on your video games or any test you take?

1020 **WYR** your daughter look up to an athlete or actress?

1021 **WYR** eat someone else's lunch at work or steal someone's lunch money?

1022 **WYR** use the other sex's restroom in an emergency or just pee outside?

1023 **WYR** always use the speaker phone option or never use speaker phone?

1024 **WYR** stop a burglary at your neighbor's house or not get involved?

1025 **WYR** live on Sesame Street or in Mister Roger's neighborhood?

1026 **WYR** dress sexy or modest?

1027 **WYR** be intimate with the lights on or off?

1028 **WYR** your spouse take your last name or you take theirs?

1029 **WYR** stop eating before you get full or when you get stuffed?

1030 **WYR** be faithful or sow your wild oats?

1031 **WYR** live in harmony or throw caution to the wind?

1032 **WYR** only brush your teeth in the morning or only at night?

1033 **WYR** live a lie to protect someone or be honest and hurt the ones around you?

1034 **WYR** spend the night in a psych ward or haunted motel?

1035 **WYR** take a vow of silence for a month or break a wedding vow on purpose?

1036 **WYR** be underestimated or under appreciated?

1037 **WYR** go on a 30 day fast from food or from music?

1038 **WYR** experience the butterfly effect or live in a constant state of déjà vu?

1039 **WYR** be a museum curator or a librarian for a year?

1040 **WYR** win a vacation or money from a raffle ticket?

1041 **WYR** have a wanderlust spirit or a protagonist spirit?

1042 **WYR** discover oil or gold on your own land?

1043 **WYR** have dinner with King Henry VIII or Kim Jong Un?

1044 **WYR** only be able to watch Netflix or only watch local network TV?

1045 **WYR** be a part of Hawaii 5-0 task force or part of the A-Team?

1046 **WYR** Gotham or Atlantis be a real place?

1047 **WYR** hang out with the Rat Pack or the Brat Pack?

1048 **WYR** go fishing with Jeremy Wade or crabbing with the crew of *Deadliest Catch*?

1049 **WYR** come across a bear or a mountain lion in the woods?

1050 **WYR** have a fruit tree or a nut tree in your backyard?

1051 **WYR** have the Transformers or Power Rangers to help defend earth?

1052 **WYR** be more soulful or more edgy?

1053 **WYR** play in The Masters or at Wimbledon?

1054 **WYR** be a warrior for a cause or for yourself?

1055 **WYR** rob a money truck or a bank?

1056 **WYR** roller rinks or arcades make a comeback?

1057 **WYR** get rid of toll roads or first-class on airplanes?

1058 **WYR** donate your body to science or donate all your organs?

1059 **WYR** chase the legend of Bigfoot or search for mermaids?

1060 **WYR** cassette tapes or jukeboxes make a comeback?

1061 **WYR** steak or cake have zero calories?

1062 **WYR** make your own pizza at home or just buy it somewhere?

1063 **WYR** peak early or later in your life?

1064 **WYR** start a movement or a revolution?

1065 **WYR** have your martini straight up or on the rocks?

1066 **WYR** eat olives or pickles?

1067 **WYR** hot apple cider or hot chocolate on a cold winter's night?

1068 **WYR** reenact a stunt from *Jackass* or *Ridiculousness*?

1069 **WYR** Steve Harvey or Arsenio Hall introduce you before a performance?

1070 **WYR** compete on *Family Feud* or *Let's Make A Deal* with your significant other?

1071 **WYR** have gallstones or kidney stones?

1072 **WYR** be addicted to your phone or social media?

1073 **WYR** drink red wine or white wine?

1074 **WYR** go out every Friday or stay home every Friday?

1075 **WYR** sing the blues or sing for your supper?

1076 **WYR** eat buffalo wings or spare ribs with sauce when wearing a white shirt?

1077 **WYR** lose your voice or your sight?

1078 **WYR** find a treasure map or find a secret message that needs decoding?

1079 **WYR** live in the world of *Zelda* or *Minecraft*?

1080 **WYR** coexist or not?

1081 **WYR** use Vaseline or Chapstick for your chapped lips?

1082 **WYR** wear stretchy pants or sweat pants?

1083 **WYR** wear tanks or tees?

1084 **WYR** get a personality or style upgrade?

1085 **WYR** be a skyscraper window washer or a dog walker picking up dog poo all day?

1086 **WYR** always follow the 5 second rule or no way?

1087 **WYR** attend a pool party or rooftop party?

1088 **WYR** have a song with good lyrics or good music?

1089 **WYR** step in animal poop or human vomit barefoot?

1090 **WYR** always be right or always get the last laugh?

1091 **WYR** have a photographic memory or exceptional problem-solving skills?

1092 **WYR** be better at math or English?

1093 **WYR** have Biggie Smalls or Tupac back from the dead?

1094 **WYR** expose all the dirty cops or dishonest politicians?

1095 **WYR** get rid of sales tax on products and services or international duty taxes?

1096 **WYR** eat only using your fingers or chopsticks?

1097 **WYR** replace fortune cookie fortunes with dirty jokes or diet tips?

1098 **WYR** be invisible for a day or be able to teleport for a day?

1099 **WYR** celebrate Christmas or Halloween all year round?

1100 **WYR** explore the Great Barrier Reef or sunken Titanic?

1101 **WYR** gamble with your life savings or your parent's life savings?

1102 **WYR** post your blog on *Wordpress* or *Blogger*?

1103 **WYR** have a show on *Animal Planet* or the *Food Network*?

1104 **WYR** go on *Dancing with the Stars* or *American Ninja Warrior*?

1105 **WYR** sing in a choir or quartet?

1106 **WYR** ban all GMO's or food dyes and colorings?

1107 **WYR** walk around covered in cake frosting or grape jelly?

1108 **WYR** be a terrible friend or terrible lover?

1109 **WYR** get busted for cheating on a test or cheating someone out of money?

1110 **WYR** be allergic to grass or dairy products?

1111 **WYR** spend the day cleaning fish or peeling potatoes?

1112 **WYR** have a bad spray tan or bad hair dye job?

1113 **WYR** more children get adopted and find families or more starving children get fed?

1114 **WYR** have a bigger master bedroom or a bigger kitchen in your new home?

1115 **WYR** have to ride a horse or a unicycle to work every day for a week?

1116 **WYR** learn more about the stock market or real estate market?

1117 **WYR** suck 10 lemons or 10 fish heads?

1118 **WYR** be a tour guide or a docent?

1119 **WYR** have a *Cosby Show* or *Brady Bunch* remake for TV?

1120 **WYR** be treated special or be treated fair?

1121 **WYR** have the perfect relationship or perfect job?

1122 **WYR** have Godiva or Hershey chocolate?

1123 **WYR** be the face of an alcoholic beverage or a cigarette brand?

1124 **WYR** join the cast of *Pitch Perfect* or *High School Rock*?

1125 **WYR** not say anything if you have nothing nice to say or just say what you want?

1126 **WYR** watch *Bad Santa* or *The Nightmare Before Christmas*?

1127 **WYR** have Clark Griswold or Noah Levenstein (*American Pie*) for a dad?

1128 **WYR** use Amazon Echo or Google Home?

1129 **WYR** slide down a sand dune or snowy hill?

1130 **WYR** give up your social life or give up everything else but your social life?

1131 **WYR** be needed or desired?

1132 **WYR** sing with Kelly Clarkson or P!nk?

1133 **WYR** never sleep in socks or always sleep in socks?

1134 **WYR** eat your nuts honey roasted or lightly salted?

1135 **WYR** snowball fight or food fight?

1136 **WYR** get a terrible wedgie or have someone moon you?

1137 **WYR** always have your teeth feel clean or always have fresh breath?

1138 **WYR** not know your worth or always know your value?

1139 **WYR** remove Charlie Sheen or O.J. Simpson from the planet?

1140 **WYR** drink iced tea or hot tea?

1141 **WYR** use lotion or coconut oil on your skin?

1142 **WYR** lie to your doctor or lie to yourself?

1143 **WYR** eat veggie chips or banana chips?

1144 **WYR** have donuts or donut holes?

1145 **WYR** move in with your mate too soon or never move in with them and they move on?

1146 **WYR** attend a drag show or a drag race?

1147 **WYR** inspire people or educate them?

1148 **WYR** clone yourself or clone your favorite pet?

1149 **WYR** always eat food that is bitter or spicy?

1150 **WYR** forget friends from your childhood or stay in contact with them?

1151 **WYR** break up with someone in person or by text?

1152 **WYR** skateboard or hoverboard through your neighborhood?

1153 **WYR** have endless hiccups or laugh until you pass out?

1154 **WYR** be diagnosed with a mental disorder or physical disorder?

1155 **WYR** have a constant tingling in your hands and feet or a constant burning in your eyes?

1156 **WYR** play an adult game of *Twister* with friends or naked hide-n-seek with neighbors?

1157 **WYR** always have your flights delayed or always be seated by annoying people on a plane?

1158 **WYR** prevent all future school shootings or all future terrorist acts?

1159 **WYR** do a ride along with a police officer or hang out at a fire station?

1160 **WYR** do all your grocery shopping only online or only in store?

1161 **WYR** eat out every day for a year or cook at home every day for a year?

1162 **WYR** lie to yourself to make you feel better or face your truth and deal with the pain?

1163 **WYR** give up shopping for new things or give up grooming for an entire year?

1164 **WYR** have hallucinations for 24 hours or experience vertigo for 48 hours?

1165 **WYR** wear a onesie or overalls all day while you're out in public?

1166 **WYR** die for a cause you believe in or die protecting strangers in a dangerous situation?

1167 **WYR** the world had giant locusts or giant crows?

1168 **WYR** pierce both eyebrows or both nostrils?

1169 **WYR** use mouthwash that tastes like vinegar or eye drops that burn like hot sauce?

1170 **WYR** have a demogorgon as a pet or the ability to change into a demogorgon?

1171 **WYR** be completely hairless all over your body or have too much hair all over your body?

1172 **WYR** send an embarrassing email to your entire family or all your co-workers?

1173 **WYR** be a cyclops or a minotaur?

1174 **WYR** eat one stick of lard (Crisco) or drink one cup of unpasteurized goat milk?

1175 **WYR** battle rap Eminem or Drake?

1176 **WYR** change humanity's chemical makeup or physical design?

1177 **WYR** eat Cadbury or Willy Wonka candies?

1178 **WYR** get rid of celebrity award shows altogether or just get rid of some?

1179 **WYR** Matthew McConaughey or Samuel Jackson read you a bedtime story?

1180 **WYR** get rid of the "National Anthem" or "Pledge of Allegiance?"

1181 **WYR** spend your extra time doing Facebook quizzes or reading listicles?

1182 **WYR** never have another good hair day or your clothes never be on point again?

1183 **WYR** always know what you want to eat or always know what your mate is thinking?

1184 **WYR** be too picky or not picky enough?

1185 **WYR** have proof we landed on the moon or proof aliens exist?

1186 **WYR** hope for the best or prepare for the worst?

1187 **WYR** eat Rice Krispies with milk as cereal or as Rice Krispies treats?

1188 **WYR** be lost in emotion or lost in translation?

1189 **WYR** lose a bet to a stranger or your best friend?

1190 **WYR** eat parsley or cilantro as a garnish?

1191 **WYR** be close with your sibling or be in competition with them?

1192 **WYR** have a funny bumper sticker or funny t-shirt?

1193 **WYR** eat string cheese or cheesecake?

1194 **WYR** jam Run DMC or Beastie Boys?

1195 **WYR** have professional portraits or take your own selfie for your profile photos?

1196 **WYR** spend more money at the Playstation store or on iTunes?

1197 **WYR** have a water view or skyline view out of your apartment?

1198 **WYR** change your name or change your personality?

1199 **WYR** flip on a trampoline or flip off a diving board?

1200 **WYR** always know what your best friend is thinking or have your own personal revelation?

1201 **WYR** live in London or Rome?

1202 **WYR** speak with an accent or never have an accent?

1203 **WYR** a stranger sneeze in your face or lick your hand?

1204 **WYR** have more time with your family or more time for yourself?

1205 **WYR** quit your job and become a waiter and live off tips or freelancer and live off odd jobs?

1206 **WYR** pull a tooth with a pair of pliers or brand yourself with a cattle prod?

1207 **WYR** always have boogers in your nose or food stuck in your front teeth?

1208 **WYR** kiss an iguana or a centipede?

1209 **WYR** write commercial jingles or theme songs to TV shows?

1210 **WYR** get pooped on by a bird 3 times a day for a week or have poison ivy for a month?

1211 **WYR** give 100 dogs a bath or milk 100 dairy cows?

1212 **WYR** have more faith in God or trust people more?

1213 **WYR** drink a glass of your significant other's blood or your own blood?

1214 **WYR** take a bath in bourbon or coffee?

1215 **WYR** your job give you a longer lunch and breaks or more employee sharing benefits?

1216 **WYR** wear cologne/perfume that smells like beer or tacos?

1217 **WYR** be tone deaf or colorblind?

1218 **WYR** wear dentures the rest of your life or have no fingernails?

1219 **WYR** break every promise you ever make to people or lie to everyone you love?

1220 **WYR** potty-train 10 puppies or 5 toddlers?

1221 **WYR** always be early or always be late?

1222 **WYR** your lotion contain menthol, or your shampoo contain mosquito repellant?

1223 **WYR** have a barbecue on the beach or on top of a mountain?

1224 **WYR** get married underwater or on top of a skyscraper?

1225 **WYR** only ever get to wear glasses or contact lenses?

1226 **WYR** have more people that love you or motivate you in your life?

1227 **WYR** run for mayor of your city or governor of your state?

1228 **WYR** have sex in a church or the back of a hearse?

1229 **WYR** play chicken with tractors or cars?

1230 **WYR** dye your hair white or gray?

1231 **WYR** mourn a death alone or with family and friends to comfort you?

1232 **WYR** read *Popular Science* or *Popular Mechanics*?

1233 **WYR** get into a spitball or pillow fight?

1234 **WYR** be exiled from society or disowned from your family?

1235 **WYR** Austin Powers or James Bond be at your service?

1236 **WYR** be eaten by Audrey from *Little Shop of Horrors* or attacked by killer tomatoes?

1237 **WYR** have a second job or one's enough?

1238 **WYR** eat dinner with your family or with your friends?

1239 **WYR** work late or get up early?

1240 **WYR** feel connected to the universe or connected to a person?

1241 **WYR** go on a road trip with Oprah or Jimmy Kimmel?

1242 **WYR** be bitten by a tiger shark or a bull shark?

1243 **WYR** visit the most beautiful beach or the most beautiful countryside in the world?

1244 **WYR** only eat Taco Bell or Subway for lunch?

1245 **WYR** eat Fun Dip or Pixie Stix?

1246 **WYR** give out money or candy to the kids in your neighborhood for Halloween?

1247 **WYR** sing "Silent Night" or "Jingle Bells" when you go caroling?

1248 **WYR** create a treasure hunt or scavenger hunt as your next big outing?

1249 **WYR** carve a pumpkin or go for a hayride this upcoming autumn?

1250 **WYR** be more afraid of water or heights?

1251 **WYR** always keep it simple or rock the boat?

1252 **WYR** bring back Whitney Houston or Aaliyah?

1253 **WYR** use only tobacco or sriracha?

1254 **WYR** always have Lo Mein noodles or fried rice with your Chinese takeout?

1255 **WYR** always avoid bad dates or block online creepers from stalking you?

1256 **WYR** make celebrities get drug tested or have salary caps per movie/show?

1257 **WYR** be Nicolas Cage in *Con Air* or *Face/Off*?

1258 **WYR** be too serious or not serious enough?

1259 **WYR** live right in the heart of a big city or out in the quiet countryside?

1260 **WYR** sleep outside for a year or sleep alone for a year?

1261 **WYR** have all your debt paid off right now or be given a new car right now?

1262 **WYR** have a praying mantis or Japanese rhinoceros beetle as a pet?

1263 **WYR** eat a raw beet or raw turnip?

1264 **WYR** be locked inside the *Big Brother* house or *Jersey Shore* house?

1265 **WYR** be conceited or shallow?

1266 **WYR** have your own clothing line or your own skin care line?

1267 **WYR** have the chance to create a smart phone app or video game?

1268 **WYR** get hit in the face by a tennis ball or football?

1269 **WYR** spend the last year of your life partying or making a difference in the world?

1270 **WYR** wear a cap or bandana on your head every day for a year?

1271 **WYR** humble yourself and become a janitor or dishwasher?

1272 **WYR** be the life of the party or fight for your right to party?

1273 **WYR** your teenager be addicted to taking selfies or candy and junk food?

1274 **WYR** spend a year living at a nudist colony or within the Amish community?

1275 **WYR** eat only Italian style food or authentic Mexican style food for an entire year?

1276 **WYR** have a baby pee or vomit on you?

1277 **WYR** have swollen lips or swollen fingers?

1278 **WYR** have to wear sock puppets on your hands or flippers on your feet?

1279 **WYR** have short-term or long-term memory loss?

1280 **WYR** save all your pennies or throw all your pennies away?

1281 **WYR** have a stray dog lick your face or get lemon juice in a really bad cut you have?

1282 **WYR** perform CPR on a baby you don't know or your elderly grandfather (chose only one)?

1283 **WYR** make your parents or your significant other take a lie detector test?

1284 **WYR** have explosive diarrhea for a week or be constipated severely for a week?

1285 **WYR** be locked in a coffin or gym locker for an hour?

1286 **WYR** drink Tang or Kool-Aid with your friends?

1287 **WYR** always buy a real Christmas tree or only use a fake Christmas tree?

1288 **WYR** have a leg or breast when you eat your chicken?

1289 **WYR** have less disappointments or less problems in your life?

1290 **WYR** eat homemade potato chips or bagged potato chips?

1291 **WYR** avoid pain or avoid stress?

1292 **WYR** people keep you guessing or just be upfront?

1293 **WYR** understand what the movie *Donnie Darko* or *Looper* is about?

1294 **WYR** be an American Psycho or a Black Swan?

1295 **WYR** attend carnivals or festivals?

1296 **WYR** only ever go to Austin City Limits or Coachella?

1297 **WYR** be an ER nurse or pediatric nurse?

1298 **WYR** be stuck on *Shutter Island* or locked inside *Inception*?

1299 **WYR** be a true believer or total skeptic?

1300 **WYR** *Game of Thrones* or *True Blood* go on forever?

1301 **WYR** do 100 jumping jacks or pushups?

1302 **WYR** be the chaperone of your kid's school dance or field trip?

1303 **WYR** be a cool or scary babysitter?

1304 **WYR** attend Dave Chappelle's or Chris Rock's next standup comedy show?

1305 **WYR** be a ghost writer who is paid well or a struggling writer waiting on a break?

1306 **WYR** feel guilty or remorseful?

1307 **WYR** achieve a higher state of enlightenment or success?

1308 **WYR** have a *Cinderella* or *Pretty Woman* fantasy?

1309 **WYR** Harvey Weinstein or Kevin Spacey go to jail?

1310 **WYR** have the most high-tech security system or two ferocious guard dogs for your home?

1311 **WYR** jump in a public fountain that says, "keep out" or pull the fire alarm at a fancy hotel?

1312 **WYR** carry a torch for someone your whole life or put out the fire?

1313 **WYR** suffer from hallucinations or paranoia?

1314 **WYR** talk to dead people or be able to predict when people are going to die?

1315 **WYR** read your original poem at a poetry slam or perform at a comedy open mic night?

1316 **WYR** be granted 10 wishes and keep them all or share half of your wishes with someone else?

1317 **WYR** have a famous parent or a famous significant other?

1318 **WYR** be able to see in the pitch-black dark or hear people's inner thoughts?

1319 **WYR** give all teachers a raise or employ more police officers throughout the world?

1320 **WYR** say everything on your mind or never say anything on your mind?

1321 **WYR** all your clothes fit you too big or too small?

1322 **WYR** swallow all the salt in your salt shaker or eat an entire bottle of horseradish?

1323 **WYR** never be able to use search engines again or never use smart phone apps again?

1324 **WYR** always have a black eye or bloody nose?

1325 **WYR** take it easy or take the lead?

1326 **WYR** always have a runny nose or a ringing in your ear?

1327 **WYR** lose your ability to be empathetic or logical?

1328 **WYR** have connections in the CIA or Interpol?

1329 **WYR** have the power of persuasion or the gift of gab?

1330 **WYR** people not take you seriously or always be afraid of you?

1331 **WYR** always have to walk in straight line or never be able to use power tools again?

1332 **WYR** abolish people trapping for furs and animal hides or abolish preservatives in all food?

1333 **WYR** lose your left leg or your right arm?

1334 **WYR** eliminate Sprite or root beer?

1335 **WYR** the government put barcodes on your wrist or microchip you?

1336 **WYR** always make the first move or never take initiative?

1337 **WYR** see Dominic Toretto or Ricky Bobby drive?

1338 **WYR** play mind games or pull heart strings?

1339 **WYR** only be able to use the opposite hand you use now or drive only using one hand?

1340 **WYR** have your family/friends perceive your significant other as a loser or liar?

1341 **WYR** be a peace maker or an instigator?

1342 **WYR** have a snowball or water balloon fight?

1343 **WYR** watch a feel-good movie or a motivational movie?

1344 **WYR** shake hands with Rosa Parks or Susan B. Anthony?

1345 **WYR** work with Nick Cannon or Nickelodeon?

1346 **WYR** own the world's most comfortable sheets or shoes?

1347 **WYR** use disposable razors or electric shavers?

1348 **WYR** have a clean bathtub or clean refrigerator at all times?

1349 **WYR** soak in a jacuzzi or relax in a sauna?

1350 **WYR** give up your gym membership or something else if you had to tighten your budget?

1351 **WYR** slow down time or speed up time?

1352 **WYR** give up hot dogs or hamburgers?

1353 **WYR** be given a Cartier or Montblanc pen?

1354 **WYR** have Raisinets or Whoppers at the movies?

1355 **WYR** chug orange or grape soda?

1356 **WYR** be called square or shady?

1357 **WYR** the world have more equality or more tolerance?

1358 **WYR** live your truth or spend more time figuring out your truth?

1359 **WYR** have more time to write or more time to read?

1360 **WYR** movies have less sequels or less remakes?

1361 **WYR** tip waiters based on service or always leave at least 15%?

1362 **WYR** eat a kale or seaweed salad?

1363 **WYR** build a man cave or she shed?

1364 **WYR** get rid of MTV or VH1?

1365 **WYR** have a sword fight or a fist fight?

1366 **WYR** spend all day listening to Pearl Jam or Nirvana?

1367 **WYR** always type or always write by hand?

1368 **WYR** eat lasagna or spaghetti?

1369 **WYR** live and let live or live and let die?

1370 **WYR** Shel Silverstein or Dr. Seuss?

1371 **WYR** be lost in the worst part of town you know or break down on an abandoned highway?

1372 **WYR** lose your ability to concentrate or lose your ability to be creative?

1373 **WYR** be an excellent cook or have a significant other that is an excellent cook?

1374 **WYR** always get the last word in an argument or always get the best seat in the house?

1375 **WYR** be too trusting or too suspicious of everyone you meet?

1376 **WYR** interview an infamous serial killer or a victim of a highly publicized crime?

1377 **WYR** throw a surprise party or have someone throw you a surprise party?

1378 **WYR** plan a family reunion or your class reunion?

1379 **WYR** work harder or work smarter?

1380 **WYR** your clothes always be itchy or wrinkly?

1381 **WYR** sit all day or stand all day at your job?

1382 **WYR** be under 5 feet tall or over 7 feet tall?

1383 **WYR** sleep with the TV on or use a nightlight?

1384 **WYR** have unwavering willpower or a high IQ score?

1385 **WYR** get revenge or forgive the last person who upset you?

1386 **WYR** eat human flesh to survive or starve to death?

1387 **WYR** be someone's first love or someone's last love?

1388 **WYR** adopt the motto "life's a beach" or "life is like a box of chocolates"?

1389 **WYR** get a shoulder massage or a foot massage?

1390 **WYR** always have a clean bathroom or clean kitchen in your home?

1391 **WYR** be a good listener or a good negotiator?

1392 **WYR** spend the day relaxing in the park or shopping at the mall?

1393 **WYR** read hardcover books or read books in digital format?

1394 **WYR** play computer games or games on a console?

1395 **WYR** marry someone who challenges you or one who is overly supportive?

1396 **WYR** eat a bar of soap or drink an entire bottle of laxative?

1397 **WYR** lick your significant other's armpit or a stranger's ear?

1398 **WYR** be the smartest person you know or the most popular in your circle of friends?

1399 **WYR** watch your enemy drown to death or bleed to death?

1400 **WYR** belong to the crew of *Mission Impossible* or *Ocean's Eleven*?

1401 **WYR** play only Parker Brothers or Hasbro games?

1402 **WYR** have a secret lover or secret admirer?

1403 **WYR** tell ghost stories or urban legends?

1404 **WYR** end bull fighting or dog fighting?

1405 **WYR** life always be fair or continue with life as we know it?

1406 **WYR** never be able to change your mind or never be able to make up your mind?

1407 **WYR** always have your car exterior clean but the interior be dirty or vice versa?

1408 **WYR** kiss face on a park bench or in a parked car?

1409 **WYR** get more exercise or get more outdoor activities?

1410 **WYR** eat out more or eat at home more?

1411 **WYR** things become more compact or more oversized?

1412 **WYR** live through *Perfect Storm* or *Armageddon*?

1413 **WYR** appreciate the people in your life more or forgive yourself more?

1414 **WYR** tell people you love them more often or find more creative outlets in your life?

1415 **WYR** Beyoncé stay married to Jay-Z or become a single lady again?

1416 **WYR** your environment have less bugs or less snakes?

1417 **WYR** avoid or embrace your current reality?

1418 **WYR** be the captain of a cruise ship or yacht?

1419 **WYR** have an endless supply of sunflower seeds or peanuts?

1420 **WYR** have muffins or scones at your next tea party?

1421 **WYR** people commit less crimes or pollute the environment less?

1422 **WYR** fish off a pier or off a boat?

1423 **WYR** dive into the deep end of a pool or float in the shallows?

1424 **WYR** sing or dance in public?

1425 **WYR** be stranded at a bus stop or airport?

1426 **WYR** perform country line dancing or the Cha Cha Slide?

1427 **WYR** build an epic sandcastle or decent treehouse?

1428 **WYR** be all knowing or have tons of materialistic things?

1429 **WYR** take a year off with pay or have a year added to your life?

1430 **WYR** be the best player on a losing team or the worst player on a winning team?

1431 **WYR** have access to your friend's medical records or get a copy of your employee file?

1432 **WYR** get shot by a nail gun or a staple gun?

1433 **WYR** your body have the perfect measurements or have the perfect IQ?

1434 **WYR** be a bounty hunter or a blue-collar worker?

1435 **WYR** be with someone who lied about their past or is currently lying to you about their job?

1436 **WYR** go on a group date or double date?

1437 **WYR** save yourself or your significant other from imminent danger?

1438 **WYR** cuddle under the stars or on the couch?

1439 **WYR** be woken up in the morning by a kiss or the smell of fresh brewed coffee?

1440 **WYR** always have to use a public toilet or only shower at your gym (nowhere else)?

1441 **WYR** live in your car for a month or live at a friend's house for a year?

1442 **WYR** always be filled with hunger or hatred?

1443 **WYR** fall in love too easily or never fall in love?

1444 **WYR** always have a clean house or always have a working car?

1445 **WYR** be too needy or too greedy?

1446 **WYR** purchase a more expensive car or a more expensive home?

1447 **WYR** be forced to shower in stilettos or wearing a life preserver?

1448 **WYR** have survivor's remorse or a lack of conscience?

1449 **WYR** have a best friend who is a genius or a billionaire?

1450 **WYR** be a survivor or a walker in *The Walking Dead*?

1451 **WYR** dress like a pimp or a gangster from the 20s?

1452 **WYR** Rudolph the Red-Nosed Reindeer or the Easter Bunny be real?

1453 **WYR** everyone believe everything you say or do everything you say?

1454 **WYR** sweat too much or cough too much?

1455 **WYR** rock Skechers or New Balance?

1456 **WYR** eat peanut butter and jelly or grilled cheese sandwiches every day?

1457 **WYR** make a mockery out of something or make a mountain out of a molehill?

1458 **WYR** buy a Sony or Samsung flat screen TV?

1459 **WYR** allow your kids to watch rated R movies or never watch them?

1460 **WYR** always have high expectations or never expect too much?

1461 **WYR** have the hookup from your waiter or cable guy?

1462 **WYR** drink from a water hose at your home or a public water fountain?

1463 **WYR** be a reporter for pop culture or politics?

1464 **WYR** read *GQ* or *Glamour*?

1465 **WYR** wear an expensive watch that doesn't tell time or a cheap watch that functions great?

1466 **WYR** do #2 in a public restroom or hold it until you get home?

1467 **WYR** watch *Grease* or *Grease 2*?

1468 **WYR** eat only Doritos or Funyuns for life?

1469 **WYR** play the cards you're dealt or forfeit the game?

1470 **WYR** take an uncharted backroad or go the familiar route?

1471 **WYR** try not to offend anyone or do what's best for you?

1472 **WYR** steal Dracula's cape or Batman's cape?

1473 **WYR** watch the original *Karate Kid* or the remake?

1474 **WYR** have French toast or pancakes for breakfast in bed?

1475 **WYR** attend a private concert where Ed Sheehan or Charlie Puth is performing?

1476 **WYR** be friends with Justin Timberlake or Justin Bieber?

1477 **WYR** listen to an acoustic or electric guitar?

1478 **WYR** have your own camel or ostrich?

1479 **WYR** be a beach bum or a vagabond?

1480 **WYR** hear a stir of echoes or see mysterious shadows?

1481 **WYR** always know what's going on or sometimes be clueless?

1482 **WYR** play the keyboard or piano?

1483 **WYR** get a road rash from falling or a really bad sunburn?

1484 **WYR** suffer from amnesia or seizures?

1485 **WYR** kiss on the cheek or French kiss on the first date?

1486 **WYR** see your neighbor or your significant other's best friend naked?

1487 **WYR** be good with kids or adults with disabilities?

1488 **WYR** live in a haunted house or live near a haunted cemetery?

1489 **WYR** the toilet clog every time you flush it or blow a fuse each time you use the microwave?

1490 **WYR** have telepathy or telekinesis?

1491 **WYR** never pay off your debt or never pay back a friend who lent you money?

1492 **WYR** the world have more amusement parks or zoos?

1493 **WYR** make your diary public or leak every secret anyone has ever told you online?

1494 **WYR** your head be too big or too small for your body?

1495 **WYR** face nuclear winter or alien invasion?

1496 **WYR** volunteer at the YMCA or SPCA?

1497 **WYR** experience a miracle or witness a shooting star?

1498 **WYR** join a bowling league or fantasy football league?

1499 **WYR** go bowling with a coconut or watermelon as your bowling ball?

1500 **WYR** have a real estate license or private detective license?

1501 **WYR** only be able to have twins if you have kids or just not have kids at all?

1502 **WYR** be a new character on the TV show *Stranger Things* or *The Walking Dead*?

1503 **WYR** live the next 5 years of your life in the wilderness of Alaska or the desert of Abu Dhabi?

1504 **WYR** snort wasabi or get a jalapeno seed stuck in your eye?

1505 **WYR** have gas or anxiety on your wedding day?

1506 **WYR** never download any new apps or never upgrade your smart phone?

1507 **WYR** change history or shape the future?

1508 **WYR** spend money travelling or a fancy car?

1509 **WYR** have an MTV Award or Nickelodeon Kid's Choice Award?

1510 **WYR** live a more luxurious or casual lifestyle?

1511 **WYR** blow all your money at casinos or on lottery tickets?

1512 **WYR** eat a salad with a worm or fake fingernail in it?

1513 **WYR** have your eyes always water or your head always itch?

1514 **WYR** be a godparent or a foster parent?

1515 **WYR** walk across a dirty parking lot or a pasture full of livestock barefoot?

1516 **WYR** have free groceries for a year or all bills paid for 6 months?

1517 **WYR** eat what you find under your sofa cushions or between the seats of your car?

1518 **WYR** co-host a morning show with Michael Strahan or Hoda Kotb?

1519 **WYR** read only *Buzzfeed's* or *Huffington Post's* blog?

1520 **WYR** make movies always have a happy ending or always leave you wondering?

1521 **WYR** cover all your food in gravy or cheese?

1522 **WYR** be in an online group for *World of Warcraft* or *Black Ops*?

1523 **WYR** face Darth Vader or Darth Maul in a lightsaber fight?

1524 **WYR** find all your missing socks or never lose your favorite pen again?

1525 **WYR** eat a plate of tofu or bowl of Vegemite?

1526 **WYR** burn incense that smells like gasoline or cheap perfume?

1527 **WYR** be called a nickname you hate or an insulting cartoon character?

1528 **WYR** eat out of a dumpster behind a restaurant or eat out of your neighbor's trash can?

1529 **WYR** go through Navy Seal or Marine Corps training?

1530 **WYR** be a one hit wonder in music or a TV show that gets cancelled after 3 episodes?

1531 **WYR** attend an authentic Hawaiian luau or Native American pow wow?

1532 **WYR** live in Canada or Mexico for a year?

1533 **WYR** bring back something from your childhood or see someone from childhood you miss?

1534 **WYR** always eat black beans or red beans?

1535 **WYR** have a comfy pillow and blanket or delicious food and drink on a long flight?

1536 **WYR** only be allowed to wear one clothing designer or one shoe designer?

1537 **WYR** your voice sound like Elmo or Kermit the Frog?

1538 **WYR** be close friends with Snoop Dog or Dr. Dre?

1539 **WYR** have kombucha or kimchi daily?

1540 **WYR** have Korean BBQ or Thai food?

1541 **WYR** be a cab driver in New York or bike messenger in Chicago?

1542 **WYR** make snow angels or a snow man in the winter?

1543 **WYR** be buried alive or painfully poisoned?

1544 **WYR** always have closure or some things are better left unknown?

1545 **WYR** eat caramel coated apples or chocolate dipper strawberries?

1546 **WYR** have a son or a daughter?

1547 **WYR** have a better attitude or better character?

1548 **WYR** spend the day with Bob Marley or Martin Luther King Jr.?

1549 **WYR** have good friends or good books?

1550 **WYR** have better judgement or stronger intuition?

1551 **WYR** see someone's potential or know how they'll make your life better?

1552 **WYR** have sorbet or ice cream sandwiches?

1553 **WYR** never say please or never say thank you?

1554 **WYR** use Gmail or Yahoo?

1555 **WYR** be an undercover snitch or a bully?

1556 **WYR** stand up for yourself or others more?

1557 **WYR** have a steak dinner or a seafood platter?

1558 **WYR** be a hyena or vulture?

1559 **WYR** inherit it all or work for everything you have?

1560 **WYR** get a hand out or a leg up?

1561 **WYR** see other's point of view or keep your own perspective intact?

1562 **WYR** visit the Philippines or Indonesia?

1563 **WYR** your mom date your best friend or the dad of your significant other?

1564 **WYR** shop Overstock.com or Wayfair.com?

1565 **WYR** be addicted to Pinterest or Twitter?

1566 **WYR** only eat French fries or tater tots?

1567 **WYR** wear your jeans inside out or your shoes on the wrong feet for a day?

1568 **WYR** have chewing gum stuck in your hair or up your nose?

1569 **WYR** have a bucket stuck on your head or your hand get stuck in a pickle jar?

1570 **WYR** be covered in fleas or ants?

1571 **WYR** have an awesome collection of something or not waste time collecting things?

1572 **WYR** a bug flies up your nose or down your throat?

1573 **WYR** wear a Christmas sweater in July or a Halloween costume at a New Year's Eve party?

1574 **WYR** have a sports car with or without a convertible top?

1575 **WYR** ride the X-Scream or Insanity at the Stratosphere in Las Vegas?

1576 **WYR** enter a contest at a county fair or compete in one of the games at a carnival?

1577 **WYR** visit Graceland or Neverland Ranch?

1578 **WYR** play the kazoo or finger cymbals?

1579 **WYR** not be able to bend your arms or legs?

1580 **WYR** have 10-inch-long fingernails or toenails?

1581 **WYR** never be able to use a calculator again or never use a ruler/tape measure ever again?

1582 **WYR** have your own minion or your own gremlin?

1583 **WYR** have a more beautiful face or more fit body than what you have now?

1584 **WYR** have less stress in your life or less responsibilities?

1585 **WYR** have more music in your life or less noise?

1586 **WYR** meet Confucius or Isaac Newton?

1587 **WYR** be more technologically inclined or better with people?

1588 **WYR** waste time or waste money?

1589 **WYR** never have to shave again or never have to style your hair again?

1590 **WYR** die by drowning or by fire?

1591 **WYR** be handcuffed all day to your crush or someone who makes you laugh?

1592 **WYR** drive backwards down a busy street or ride a bike down a huge hill blindfolded?

1593 **WYR** use a pogo stick on an icy lake or ride a wild horse without a saddle?

1594 **WYR** have the winning hand at a major poker tournament or the keys to happiness?

1595 **WYR** have fangs and claws or wings?

1596 **WYR** have a cooking showdown against Bobby Flay or Curtis Stone?

1597 **WYR** have a walk of shame or see your nemesis do a walk of shame?

1598 **WYR** be a shape shifter or be able to manipulate water?

1599 **WYR** have the ability to decode and cypher any encryption or be an elite code writer?

1600 **WYR** surround yourself with people who party all the time or pursue their dreams?

1601 **WYR** be in business with *The Godfather* or *Scarface*?

1602 **WYR** always make a bad first impression or never leave a lasting impression?

1603 **WYR** be enemies with The Punisher or Robin Hood?

1604 **WYR** have insomnia or amnesia for a month?

1605 **WYR** give up donuts or pizza forever?

1606 **WYR** kill in self-defense or kill in revenge?

1607 **WYR** have rice thrown or doves released at your wedding?

1608 **WYR** become a famous architect or an important astronomer?

1609 **WYR** be a local news anchor or a national weather forecaster?

1610 **WYR** soak in the Dead Sea or the mineral rich mud baths at Calistoga Springs?

1611 **WYR** kiss the Blarney Stone in Ireland or visit Balzac's house in Paris?

1612 **WYR** improvise and use a trash can or bucket as a toilet?

1613 **WYR** write reviews for Yelp or Google?

1614 **WYR** be the spokesperson for a hemorrhoid cream or face of an adult diaper brand?

1615 **WYR** own a jet ski or snow ski?

1616 **WYR** drink a glass full of raw eggs or eat 10 cans of Spam?

1617 **WYR** have more passion or more trust in your relationship?

1618 **WYR** perform singing telegrams or be a wedding singer?

1619 **WYR** play 20 questions or truth or dare with a stranger?

1620 **WYR** play on a roller derby or ice hockey team?

1621 **WYR** work the roulette wheel or blackjack table in Las Vegas?

1622 **WYR** have a lazy coworker or a lazy spouse?

1623 **WYR** fly on Air Force One or ride first class on the best airline in the world?

1624 **WYR** rappel down the Statue of Liberty or Eiffel Tower?

1625 **WYR** get stuck in the cargo hold of an airplane or restroom the entire flight?

1626 **WYR** visit the largest mall in the world or The Coliseum?

1627 **WYR** learn tap from Savion Glover or learn how to croon from Michael Bublé?

1628 **WYR** get a paper cut on your tongue or your eyelid?

1629 **WYR** have a self-cleaning toilet or car?

1630 **WYR** bring back the TV show *Seinfeld* or *Friends*?

1631 **WYR** own a coffee shop or auto repair garage?

1632 **WYR** burn bridges or keep your enemies close?

1633 **WYR** think outside the box or color outside the lines of life?

1634 **WYR** pull a flash mob in a movie theater or in the middle of a restaurant?

1635 **WYR** be questioned about your motives or your integrity?

1636 **WYR** share your wealth with your kids or let them make their own money?

1637 **WYR** be called weird or rude?

1638 **WYR** Camelot or Sleepy Hollow be a real place today?

1639 **WYR** Photoshop or use filters on all your selfies?

1640 **WYR** be raised by a pack of wolves or a tribe of gorillas?

1641 **WYR** be allergic to people or allergic to everything but people?

1642 **WYR** driving or voting age be moved to 21 years of age?

1643 **WYR** have an outbreak of bedbugs or fleas in your home?

1644 **WYR** go through life feeling guilty or with a chip on your shoulder?

1645 **WYR** eat 100 raw oysters or gourmet prepared cow tongue?

1646 **WYR** have the ability to change into another animal or assume another person's identity?

1647 **WYR** find Waldo or explore with Dora?

1648 **WYR** play with Legos or tinker toys right now?

1649 **WYR** have a driving license that never expires or tires that never go flat?

1650 **WYR** have double vision or suffer from blackouts?

1651 **WYR** have a premonition or omen?

1652 **WYR** get recruited by *The Lost Boys* or *The Outsiders*?

1653 **WYR** be a hippie or hipster?

1654 **WYR** eat Lemonheads or listen to Lemonheads?

1655 **WYR** have a Drumstick or Klondike bar?

1656 **WYR** have strawberry shortcake or crème brûlée for dessert?

1657 **WYR** play football in the park or frisbee at the beach?

1658 **WYR** throw confetti or glitter?

1659 **WYR** shine bright like a diamond or wear the diamonds?

1660 **WYR** be in *Blade* or *Underworld*?

1661 **WYR** do a skit with Jordan Peele or Keegan-Michael Key?

1662 **WYR** bring back *All That* or *In Living Color*?

1663 **WYR** be the life of the party or a good conversationalist?

1664 **WYR** have animal crackers or graham crackers?

1665 **WYR** your computer or smartphone never crash again?

1666 **WYR** follow advice from your parents or the good book?

1667 **WYR** have Charlie Brown or Snoopy as a pal?

1668 **WYR** eat snow cones or popsicles?

1669 **WYR** get back wasted time or get back wasted energy?

1670 **WYR** make the world have one currency or one language?

1671 **WYR** never pay taxes or never pay tuition again?

1672 **WYR** have a shingles outbreak or heat stroke?

1673 **WYR** apply the *48 Laws of Power* or *The Art of War* principles to your life?

1674 **WYR** have an endless hangover or endless cough?

1675 **WYR** cheer other people up or always have someone around to cheer you up?

1676 **WYR** have spearmint or peppermint gum?

1677 **WYR** smoke a pipe or chew tobacco?

1678 **WYR** have a granny smith or red delicious apple a day?

1679 **WYR** be trapped in a bizarre love triangle or be the focus of a stalker?

1680 **WYR** have horrible body odor that deodorant didn't help or severe halitosis?

1681 **WYR** figure out the meaning of life or figure out your life's purpose?

1682 **WYR** be a chief of police or chief of the fire department?

1683 **WYR** make a tiny home out of a school bus or a shipping container?

1684 **WYR** have a TV sitcom or movie be made about your life?

1685 **WYR** eat the most expensive dessert or drink the most expensive champagne in the world?

1686 **WYR** drink castor oil or baking soda and water?

1687 **WYR** see a remake of *Mary Poppins* or *The Sound of Music*?

1688 **WYR** get rid of the TV show *Keeping Up with the Kardashians* or *Catfish*?

1689 **WYR** only be allowed to shop at Ikea or Walmart for your household décor and furniture?

1690 **WYR** go on *The Tonight Show Starring Jimmy Fallon* or *The Late Late Show with James Corden?*

1691 **WYR** have Adele or John Legend sing at your wedding?

1692 **WYR** have a highlight reel of your life so far played for your parents or your significant other?

1693 **WYR** get drunk and do something stupid or something you'll regret?

1694 **WYR** be a defendant in civil or criminal court?

1695 **WYR** have back spasms or a slipped disc in your back?

1696 **WYR** lose control or lose your faith?

1697 **WYR** put all your eggs in one basket or count your chickens before they hatch?

1698 **WYR** have an herb garden or vegetable garden?

1699 **WYR** children play sports or be more academic?

1700 **WYR** be handcuffed or zip tied?

1701 **WYR** have someone rock your world or knock your socks off?

1702 **WYR** confide in your parents or best friend?

1703 **WYR** see the end of Earth or the birth of a new civilization?

1704 **WYR** be told you look older or younger than you are?

1705 **WYR** get licked in the face by a dog or a toddler?

1706 **WYR** find a hidden tunnel or hidden room in your house?

1707 **WYR** read gospel hymn books or movie soundtrack lyrics?

1708 **WYR** exaggerate or under estimate?

1709 **WYR** take a leap of faith or wish upon a star?

1710 **WYR** have Dumbledore's or Gandalf's power?

1711 **WYR** work at the grocery store or a fast food restaurant the rest of your life?

1712 **WYR** have a long-lost sibling and meet them or prefer not to know?

1713 **WYR** watch a video compilation of your life's greatest victories or stupidest moments?

1714 **WYR** have pink eyes or purple eyebrows?

1715 **WYR** have maple syrup or honey?

1716 **WYR** play tug of war or flag football at your next family reunion?

1717 **WYR** have biscuits or toast with breakfast?

1718 **WYR** be a know-it-all or a smartass?

1719 **WYR** have an unlimited new movie subscription or new video game subscription?

1720 **WYR** listen to Michael Bublé or Frank Sinatra?

1721 **WYR** know all the skeletons in your dad's or mom's closet?

1722 **WYR** be a school bus driver or principal for a day?

1723 **WYR** be able to make it rain or snow?

1724 **WYR** live large or love long?

1725 **WYR** your doctor be the same sex as you or opposite sex?

1726 **WYR** be humble and kind or boisterous and rude?

1727 **WYR** lose the ability to get road rage or depressed?

1728 **WYR** pee in the swimming pool or get out and pee?

1729 **WYR** make fun of other people or make fun of yourself?

1730 **WYR** seek advice or ask for help?

1731 **WYR** prove your critics wrong or silence your haters?

1732 **WYR** wipe ants off your food at a picnic or dust mold off your bread?

1733 **WYR** McDonald's or Burger King go out of business?

1734 **WYR** invest in people going places or new technology stocks?

1735 **WYR** your spouse be driven and hardworking or totally faithful (they can't be both)?

1736 **WYR** live right next door to your parents or 1,000 miles away?

1737 **WYR** have a mentor or figure things out on your own?

1738 **WYR** log roll yourself down a hill or leap frog over fire hydrants for an entire day?

1739 **WYR** focus on staying in shape or furthering your career (you can't do both)?

1740 **WYR** get rid of mosquitos or moths?

1741 **WYR** rent a Hummer or Porsche Cayenne limo for your birthday bash?

1742 **WYR** own a vacation home in the mountains or at the beach?

1743 **WYR** get rid of all dollar stores or all fast food chains?

1744 **WYR** study for your real estate license or for the Bar examination to practice law?

1745 **WYR** have 24 hours of playtime life on *Candy Crush Saga* or original *Flappy Birds*?

1746 **WYR** drink a gallon of Ovaltine or Gatorade?

1747 **WYR** invest in a race horse or peer-to-peer lending?

1748 **WYR** give up candy for Halloween or turkey for Thanksgiving?

1749 **WYR** get rid of hiccups or cellulite forever?

1750 **WYR** be a silent partner in your parent's business or your significant other's business?

1751 **WYR** be an optimist or realist?

1752 **WYR** help out on GoFundMe or Kickstarter?

1753 **WYR** a chimpanzee gives you a massage or clip your toe nails?

1754 **WYR** toilet paper your parents' house or your in-laws' house?

1755 **WYR** know why the chicken crossed the road or what the fox says?

1756 **WYR** run from a pack of dogs holding steaks or run from one bear while covered in honey?

1757 **WYR** wear mops on your feet or sponges on your hands?

1758 **WYR** eat mangos or papayas?

1759 **WYR** learn how to play the harp or take up rock polishing?

1760 **WYR** ride a mechanical bull or a real bull?

1761 **WYR** put your overweight child on a diet or have them do more outdoor activities?

1762 **WYR** never be allowed to use toilet paper or soap again?

1763 **WYR** know your role or break the mold?

1764 **WYR** never have competition or always compete against the best?

1765 **WYR** give mouth-to-mouth resuscitation to a snake or raccoon?

1766 **WYR** be a Teenage Mutant Ninja Turtle or Thundercat?

1767 **WYR** have more ah-ha moments or more butterfly in the stomach moments?

1768 **WYR** your house smell like vinegar or ammonia?

1769 **WYR** have a nosebleed that won't stop or live in a room that won't stop spinning?

1770 **WYR** have extra wide feet or super narrow feet?

1771 **WYR** climb trees like a monkey or run as fast as a cheetah?

1772 **WYR** eat chicken hearts or cow liver?

1773 **WYR** be an outcast with integrity or part of a clique with no morals?

1774 **WYR** take the violence out of all music or allow freedom of creativity no matter how violent?

1775 **WYR** have goat milk or buttermilk on your breakfast cereal?

1776 **WYR** put googly eye stickers on everything in your mom's refrigerator or put up a for sale sign?

1777 **WYR** have Dr. Jekyll or Dr. Frank-N-Furter experiment on you?

1778 **WYR** be Scorpion or Sub-Zero from *Mortal Kombat*?

1779 **WYR** have carpet or no carpet in your next home?

1780 **WYR** run an obstacle course or ride in a chariot race?

1781 **WYR** have more people or more things in your life?

1782 **WYR** have VIP or executive status?

1783 **WYR** have more grace or be shown more mercy?

1784 **WYR** change the present or future?

1785 **WYR** get lost at sea or lost in the jungle?

1786 **WYR** have the ability to hibernate like a bear or chew through things like a beaver?

1787 **WYR** lower your expectations or raise your standards?

1788 **WYR** feel motion sickness or physical fatigue?

1789 **WYR** be a competitive champion or a champion for the human race?

1790 **WYR** eliminate paper products or eliminate emissions to save the environment?

1791 **WYR** wear a lit birthday cake or bird's nest with eggs on your head?

1792 **WYR** have to make your own homemade butter or never eat butter or margarine again?

1793 **WYR** be a backup dancer for Jennifer Lopez or backup singer for Bruno Mars?

1794 **WYR** have someone in your life that's a burden or you be a burden to someone else?

1795 **WYR** brew your own beer or moonshine?

1796 **WYR** have an extra set of eyebrows on your forehead or a very hairy unibrow (no trimming!)?

1797 **WYR** drink out of your pet's water dish or a glass of ocean water?

1798 **WYR** mow/cut your grass with scissors or a machete?

1799 **WYR** eat a bowl of spoiled caviar or 2 spoonsful of tadpoles?

1800 **WYR** have 3 hours less or 3 hours more of sunlight each day?

1801 **WYR** draw comic books or build robots?

1802 **WYR** have a *Night at the Museum* or *Romancing the Stone* adventure?

1803 **WYR** serve food or alcohol at your wedding reception (you can't serve both)?

1804 **WYR** have a mounted moose head or a bear head as the centrepiece of your living room?

1819 **WYR** change human nature or society's standards?

1820 **WYR** be irreplaceable or irresistible?

1821 **WYR** try roast rattlesnake or sautéed fish heads?

1822 **WYR** know others' current intentions or know their full intention?

1823 **WYR** have more intelligent or more kind people on Earth?

1824 **WYR** live a healthy life or purposeful life?

1825 **WYR** waste your potential or waste an opportunity?

1826 **WYR** eat fruit roll-ups or gummy bears?

1827 **WYR** people call you boring or a slacker?

1828 **WYR** subscribe to the motto "the more the merrier" or "three's a crowd"?

1829 **WYR** see your future self or revisit your child self?

1830 **WYR** learn more about the universe or human psyche?

1831 **WYR** history or math be obsolete?

1832 **WYR** happiness or hope be sold in vending machines?

1805 **WYR** eat a cheesecake where the main ingredient is flowers or some healthy green algae?

1806 **WYR** your life looks like the plot from *Sausage Party* or *Ratatouille*?

1807 **WYR** eat dinner with your online stalker or your ex from your worst relationship?

1808 **WYR** get rid of pop tarts or waffles?

1809 **WYR** send your child to a private school or a charter school?

1810 **WYR** a professional league for Lacrosse or Rugby get developed on the scale of the NFL?

1811 **WYR** your glasses have built in cleaning fluid with wiper blades or automatic defrosters?

1812 **WYR** walk around with a ball and chain on your leg or wear a sympathy belly for a week?

1813 **WYR** get lifestyle advice from Gwyneth Paltrow or Martha Stewart?

1814 **WYR** own and operate a food truck or petting zoo?

1815 **WYR** get rid of the iron and ironing board or feather dusters?

1816 **WYR** have a fish tank or sound machine next to your bed?

1817 **WYR** have Ozzie Osbourne or Metallica perform at your next birthday party?

1818 **WYR** share our planet with trolls or pikachus?

1833 **WYR** design a new car or create a new safety invention?

1834 **WYR** see more celebrity gossip or less celebrity gossip?

1835 **WYR** society be more advanced or less dependent on "things?"

1836 **WYR** have cherry or apple pie?

1837 **WYR** never compromise or be open to compromise?

1838 **WYR** a car run over your foot or get kicked by a donkey?

1839 **WYR** have friends with the same ideals or beliefs?

1840 **WYR** have warts on your fingers or cysts on your eyelids?

1841 **WYR** be a great storyteller or convincing liar?

1842 **WYR** broaden your horizon or broaden your audience?

1843 **WYR** date an atheist or racist?

1844 **WYR** your skin feels slimy or bumpy?

1845 **WYR** gain insight or gain ground in your life?

1846 **WYR** your yawn sound like a lawnmower or your cough sound like a seal barking?

1847 **WYR** own 10 baby goats or a bonsai tree farm?

1848 **WYR** experience purple rain or chocolate rain?

1849 **WYR** write children's books or instruction manuals?

1850 **WYR** pick Nancy Drew or Veronica Mars when it comes to solving a mysterious crime?

1851 **WYR** play Sudoku or *NY Times* crossword puzzles all day?

1852 **WYR** be more modern or more traditional?

1853 **WYR** be the detectives from *The X-Files* or *Law & Order: SVU?*

1854 **WYR** drive a creepy ice cream truck or the Oscar Mayer Wiener mobile everywhere you go?

1855 **WYR** have to bedazzle all your jeans or sew decals on all your shirts?

1856 **WYR** drink food coloring straight from the bottle or eat candle wax as it's melting?

1857 **WYR** always be in a hurry or never have a sense of urgency?

1858 **WYR** have your sofa covered in pet hair or a noisy plastic cover if you can't take either off?

1859 **WYR** the night stars be your guide or follow an actual compass?

1860 **WYR** your cellphone break or tooth crack while you're driving?

1861 **WYR** actually see a phoenix rising or the transformation process of a werewolf?

1862 **WYR** lose your ability to read or lose your ability to write?

1863 **WYR** shoot all your friends with a super soaker filled with squid ink or smelly clam juice?

1864 **WYR** only be allowed to drink coconut water or cactus juice?

1865 **WYR** drive your friends around on a Zamboni or John Deer tractor?

1866 **WYR** find a land of giants or a land of people small as mice?

1867 **WYR** have the Hulk or the Thing help you fight your battles?

1868 **WYR** have Wonder Woman or Erin Brockovich as your mother?

1869 **WYR** almost get hit by lightning or a car while walking?

1870 **WYR** get a rope burn or splattered with hot grease?

1871 **WYR** see a hip-hop rap concert with your grandmother or mother-in-law?

1872 **WYR** travel the world alone or with someone?

1873 **WYR** follow the Yellow Brick Road or follow The White Rabbit?

1874 **WYR** relive one of your best days all over again or redo one of your worst days ever?

1875 **WYR** it taste like onions or pickles each time you burp?

1876 **WYR** hear gossip about a co-worker or family member?

1877 **WYR** be locked overnight in a department store or amusement park?

1878 **WYR** always hear a clock ticking or church bells in your ear?

1879 **WYR** marry for money or love?

1880 **WYR** face a fork in the road or be forced to pick between 3 doors?

1881 **WYR** be someone's muse or discover your own muse?

1882 **WYR** have friends more like you or opposite of you?

1883 **WYR** visit the Netherworld from *Beetlejuice* or sunken place from *Get Out*?

1884 **WYR** burp bubbles or fart green fumes?

1885 **WYR** spray can cheese or can whip cream down your throat?

1886 **WYR** eat a jar of baby food or kiss a frog?

1887 **WYR** take a magic pill that will make you smarter or more attractive to others?

1888 **WYR** know a secret that could get you killed or accidentally lose a million-dollar idea?

1889 **WYR** live somewhere it's always windy or no wind at all ever?

1890 **WYR** be more aggressive or more passive?

1891 **WYR** only use hand sanitizer or only be able to use soap and water to clean your hands?

1892 **WYR** always hear birds chirping or always smell fresh flowers out your window?

1893 **WYR** only be allowed to eat the toppings off pizza or only allowed to eat crust?

1894 **WYR** drink only floats or milkshakes?

1895 **WYR** clean up trash along the highway or clean up litter on the beach?

1896 **WYR** have thumb tacks on the end of your fingers or paperclips on the end of your toes?

1897 **WYR** live a glamorous or meaningful life?

1898 **WYR** drink Coke with chocolate syrup or Pepsi with vanilla syrup?

1899 **WYR** eat all your food super spicy or bland?

1900 **WYR** take a writing or self-defense class?

1901 **WYR** live like the Flintstones or Jetsons?

1902 **WYR** chicken noodle soup or NyQuil when you don't feel well?

1903 **WYR** watch your TV shows as they air, or binge watch all your shows?

1904 **WYR** try Weight Watchers or paleo lifestyle if you needed to lose weight?

1905 **WYR** have the perfect weekend or a good week at work?

1906 **WYR** always hang out with a group of friends or hang out with one special friend?

1907 **WYR** find an alligator or an alligator snapping turtle on your front porch?

1908 **WYR** always keep your phone on vibrate or always keep the ringer on (one or the other)?

1909 **WYR** have a brush with death or get a fishing lure caught on your face?

1910 **WYR** be able to explore a volcano or newly discovered ancient ruins?

1911 **WYR** live in doubt or live in fear?

1912 **WYR** always feel rested or always feel motivated?

1913 **WYR** potato sack race or three-legged race?

1914 **WYR** have the ability to control machines or control electricity?

1915 **WYR** have invincibility or immortality?

1916 **WYR** not be afraid of dying or not be afraid of living up to your full potential?

1917 **WYR** plant rose bushes or fruit trees around your home?

1918 **WYR** be a humanitarian or philanthropist?

1919 **WYR** have a magic button that erases songs you hate or bad movies from being released?

1920 **WYR** take a step back and reflect or leap two steps forward?

1921 **WYR** eat tootsie pops or jolly ranchers?

1922 **WYR** have your snot thick like tree sap or eye boogers like applesauce?

1923 **WYR** people have more patience with each other or more wisdom in their actions?

1924 **WYR** a spouse that cooks great or stays physically fit?

1925 **WYR** have only fried or only baked food?

1926 **WYR** be a big fish in a small pond or a small fish in a big pond?

1927 **WYR** drink homemade lemonade or fresh squeezed orange juice?

1928 **WYR** have an annoying ringtone or embarrassing screensaver?

1929 **WYR** never face consequences or challenges?

1930 **WYR** increase human life span or increase quality of life for humans?

1931 **WYR** lose all the money you have in the bank right now or lose all your friends?

1932 **WYR** have your own personal manicurist or car detailer?

1933 **WYR** have more confidence or more friends?

1934 **WYR** love yourself more or be able to open up to other people more?

1935 **WYR** have the discipline of a ballerina or the focus of a skilled surgeon?

1936 **WYR** have the chance to attend Julliard or Harvard?

1937 **WYR** eat hoagies or gyros?

1938 **WYR** be forced to live underground or as a recluse the rest of your life?

1939 **WYR** hang out with Winnie the Pooh or Curious George?

1940 **WYR** have a missed opportunity or miss a chance at love?

1941 **WYR** get a do over with a person or a second chance at a past mistake?

1942 **WYR** have eight arms like an octopus or the all-seeing Eye of Providence?

1943 **WYR** get a chance to meet Hercules or Cleopatra?

1944 **WYR** live with Aborigine people or a Zulu tribe for a week?

1945 **WYR** have a hen that lays golden eggs or a money tree?

1946 **WYR** eat hummus or tzatziki?

1947 **WYR** get lost in the world of *The NeverEnding Story* or *The Secret of NIMH*?

1948 **WYR** eat only salty food or only sweet food for a year?

1949 **WYR** people constantly gossip about you or never notice you at all?

1950 **WYR** make sacrifices for people you love or only for yourself?

1951 **WYR** try your hand at glass blowing or making pottery?

1952 **WYR** make a few changes to your current life or create a whole new one?

1953 **WYR** have more happiness in your day or more energy to get through your day?

1954 **WYR** have a school or a street named after you?

1955 **WYR** have all your problems solved or have one of your dreams come true?

1956 **WYR** have more technology or less technology in your life?

1957 **WYR** have your entire house or your car completely touch screen?

1958 **WYR** play in a mariachi band or a jug band for one day?

1959 **WYR** never wear gold or never wear silver again?

1960 **WYR** work in an office that's too bright or too dark?

1961 **WYR** have a celebrity personal trainer or your own life coach?

1962 **WYR** Stan Lee or Jackie Chan direct a fight scene you're in?

1963 **WYR** look better in pictures or better in person?

1964 **WYR** have constant brain freeze or teeth chattering?

1965 **WYR** squish a spider under your bare foot or have a frog pee on your head?

1966 **WYR** double your life span or cut your enemy's life span in half?

1967 **WYR** be allergic to rain or sunshine?

1968 **WYR** act without thinking or think without acting?

1969 **WYR** have more good habits or more education?

1970 **WYR** have unlimited access to Warren Buffet or Charles Koch for advice?

1971 **WYR** sing in the shower or sing in the rain?

1972 **WYR** ride in a paddle boat with your sweetie or stand up paddle board together?

1973 **WYR** be more like a kid again or more polished and mature?

1974 **WYR** read more books or watch less TV?

1975 **WYR** eat a piece of raw meat or swallow 10 pieces of gum?

1976 **WYR** be sharp as cheddar or cool as ice?

1977 **WYR** only be able to eat with a fork or only with a spoon?

1978 **WYR** have Scooby Doo or Garfield as a pet?

1979 **WYR** slave away at a job 9-5 or hustle on your own 24/7?

1980 **WYR** have your significant other or one of your parents as your best friend?

1981 **WYR** have superfast reading or typing ability?

1982 **WYR** have the prose of Robert Frost or creativity of Maya Angelou?

1983 **WYR** lose feeling in your legs or arms for a week?

1984 **WYR** have a useless talent or no talent at all?

1985 **WYR** come across Hogzilla or the legendary Irish elk on your next camping trip?

1986 **WYR** someone give you a reality check or a hug every day?

1987 **WYR** sell all of your possessions in a garage sale or donate them to people?

1988 **WYR** have 5 international plane tickets or 20 domestic plane tickets?

1989 **WYR** eat ice cream or pudding with your hands?

1990 **WYR** have a vintage Vespa in mint condition or vintage designer couture?

1991 **WYR** movie theaters have better food or more comfortable seats?

1992 **WYR** take a vacation away from people or have a huge family vacation?

1993 **WYR** always hope for the best or prepare for the worst (you only get one)?

1994 **WYR** be a whistleblower or a confidential informant?

1995 **WYR** only be allowed to write in calligraphy or round hand?

1996 **WYR** have revenge or justice?

1997 **WYR** try sumo wrestling or capoeira?

1998 **WYR** have your home be wall-to-wall mirrors or glow-in-the-dark paint?

1999 **WYR** retire in Hawaii or where you live right now?

2000 **WYR** bite an uncooked potato or Brussels sprout?